Awakening Beauty
the Dr. Hauschka Way

Awakening Beauty
the Dr. Hauschka Way

Susan West Kurz
with Tom Monte

CLAIRVIEW

Clairview Books
Hillside House, The Square
Forest Row, East Sussex
RH18 5ES

www.clairviewbooks.com

Published in the United Kingdom by
Clairview Books 2006

A catalogue record for this book is available
from the British Library

ISBN-13: 978 1 905570 03 4
ISBN-10: 1 905570 03 1

Design by Jennifer K. Beal
Printed in the United States of America

contents

Introduction   7

Chapter 1
Restoring Beauty with
Rhythm   14

Chapter 2
The Healing Power of
Plants   34

Chapter 3
The Skin   52

Chapter 4
The Face   64

Chapter 5
Healing Specific Skin
Conditions   94

Chapter 6
Alchemy: Transforming Your
Inner and Outer Beauty   104

Chapter 7
Practicing Beauty   118

Chapter 8
Sustainable Beauty: How Beauty
Affects Our World   140

Chapter 9
Menus and Recipes for
Healthy and Beautiful
Skin   144

Acknowledgments   202
Index   203
Index of Recipes   207
Photo Credits   208

Introduction

"If only you would smile, you would be beautiful," my mother sometimes said to me when I was a young girl. As I grew older, other adults continued to point out characteristics that if changed would make me more beautiful. Eventually, I took over the job of critiquing my appearance. I often told myself that if my nose were straighter, or my eyes less deep-set, or my hips a little smaller, I would indeed be beautiful.

I emerged from childhood unable to see my beauty. And because I couldn't see it, I couldn't appreciate being me. You could say that my perception of my beauty—and my relationship to myself—was diminished or even wounded.

As I matured, I came to realize that I was not alone. Most of my peers—even those whom I considered beautiful by any standard—were often unable to see and appreciate their beauty.

Recently, I asked a few very attractive women if they considered themselves beautiful. One told me, "Oh no, I'm not beautiful. Are you kidding?" Another said, "People tell me I'm beautiful, but I don't feel beautiful." Yet another woman answered by asking, "Do you think I'm beautiful?" "Yes, I do," I said. She hugged me, and when we let go of each other, I could see tears in her eyes.

It took me many years to heal something fundamental inside myself so that I could recognize and be grateful for my beauty. As I came to know myself, I eventually realized that beauty is a luminous and joyful state of self-love that lives inside all of us. This inner beauty has the power to affect our outer beauty by improving the health of our skin, transforming the shape and movement of our bodies, and giving off a radiance that inspires those around us. As Oscar Wilde once wrote, "One does not see anything until one sees its beauty." That's especially true when applied to ourselves.

As a society, our relationship with beauty is in crisis. We are told that beauty exists only in certain images and only at certain ages. The media assault us with images that lead us away from our own unique beauty. They encourage us to try to look like someone else rather than become and accept more of who we truly are. While adults suffer from such messages, they are especially damaging to children, who want so desperately to be loved, approved of, and seen as beautiful.

Equally damaging is the message that beauty is unattainable beyond a certain age. We worship youth and deny the aging process, even though young people are often inexperienced, immature, full of conflict, and lacking in emotional depth. We are often unable to see the beauty in spiritual growth, maturity, and wisdom. As I show later in this book, each stage of life offers us unique opportunities to experience our own inner and outer beauty.

This book is about healing your inner and outer beauty. By adopting the healing and lifestyle practices I recommend, you will see and experience both your inner and outer beauty; you will nourish and develop it; and you will see it come shining forth.

Healing the Skin

A big part of healing your inner beauty is healing your skin and restoring its health, vitality, and glow. I have been working in the skin care and beauty industry for the past twenty-five years. I have been an esthetician, a teacher of skin care, a businesswoman, and, today, the president of Dr. Hauschka Skin Care, Inc. Over the course of that quarter-century, I have learned a great deal about what the skin needs to be healthy and beautiful. Unfortunately, many of today's products do more harm than good or simply address symptoms without restoring the skin's underlying health and function.

No other organ is so intimately connected to our appearance and our beauty than our skin. When we damage our skin, we diminish our beauty and change the way we feel about ourselves overall. Therefore, healing our skin is an essential part of healing our beauty.

Rudolf Hauschka developed essential principles to address healthy skin and healing beauty. A twentieth-century Austrian chemist, Dr. Hauschka created a company in the 1950s whose goals were to heal humanity and the earth. Hauschka wanted to create a new form of medicine, one that healed illness and its symptoms but also restored the health and function of the overall organism without damaging side effects. Medicine should treat the entire person, Hauschka believed, by boosting the body's healing forces, including the subtle energies that animate it and restore its health. After twenty years of trial and error, Hauschka developed a method of extracting plants' active ingredients as well as their vital energies. He then began supplying these plant-based medicines to doctors and healers throughout Europe, with remarkable results.

In the 1960s, he was joined by Austrian-born esthetician Elisabeth Sigmund, who specialized in creating medicinal substances that healed the skin and restored its underlying functions, such as its capacity to replenish cells and keep its underlying fibers moist and full. By creating such healing formulas, Sigmund hoped to incorporate skin care into mainstream medicine.

Together, Hauschka and Sigmund created a line of herbal medicine skin care products. Each is made from high-potency medicinal plants that have been grown biodynamically. (Biodynamics is a form of agriculture that far exceeds organic standards in its purity and reverence for nature.) The plants are harvested by hand at dawn, when their essential oils and life energies are strongest. They are processed using Hauschka's rhythmical extraction method, which preserves and enhances the plants' vital forces. This combination of medicinal properties and botanicals has a powerful healing effect on the skin.

I was first introduced to the Dr. Hauschka Skin Care products and philosophy in 1972, when I apprenticed at the Meadowbrook Herb Garden in Rhode Island, where I learned to grow medicinal and culinary herbs for food, medicine, and cosmetics. The man who guided me in this work imported and sold the Dr. Hauschka Skin Care line. It wasn't long before I became an independent sales representative, initially selling Dr. Hauschka to friends and family, including my boyfriend, later my husband, actor J. T. Walsh.

above Author Susan Kurz was introduced to Dr. Hauschka Skin Care products and philosophy in 1972.

below Austrian chemist Dr. Rudolf Hauschka (1891–1969) cofounded WALA Heilmittel in Eckwälden, Germany—a company whose goals were to heal humanity and the earth.

opposite Elisabeth Sigmund, groundbreaking esthetician and cofounder of Dr. Hauschka Skin Care, developed products and treatments to inspire beauty by supporting health.

Before appearing in movies, J. T. acted on the stage, where his sensitive Irish skin was subjected each night to harsh makeup and hot lights. He suffered constantly from a variety of skin problems.

Using the Dr. Hauschka principles and training as my guide, I set up an intensive treatment program for him that included healing skin care applications, herbal teas, and organic food. It wasn't long before his skin was both healthy and glowing. Later, J. T. worked with well-known makeup artist Leslie Fuller, who studied the Dr. Hauschka methods and used them to care for his skin before and after applying his makeup. Leslie, like many Hollywood makeup artists, introduced the Dr. Hauschka products and principles to other film stars. A-list celebrities, professional makeup artists, and Hollywood stylists have long embraced Dr. Hauschka's botanical products, attracted by their extraordinary results and the company's thirty-five-year commitment to purity, therapy, and luxury.

Guided by the Dr. Hauschka principles, I am going to show you how to choose skin care products that, when combined with other healing behaviors, can restore the beauty of your skin and heal it of disorders from which it may suffer, including acne, rosacea, and premature aging. In many cases, I will show you how to create your own powerful herbal formulations from plant-based ingredients that are inexpensive and easily obtainable. By using these recommendations, you can transform your appearance and restore the glow and beauty to your skin.

The Dr. Hauschka way is more than a medicinal approach to the skin, or what you put on your face. It offers practical guidance for slowing down, finding your natural rhythms, and discovering the true inner beauty that already lives inside you.

The skin, like all your organs, is infused with an energy that permeates its cells and gives it health and beauty. That underlying life force, if you will, is intimately connected to your inner beauty. If you allow yourself, you can perceive this underlying life force when you touch your face. The connection between your hands and your spirit is so strong that it makes you forget the skin of your face or the bones beneath the skin. By enhancing your connection to your inner life, your beauty can be experienced—first by you, and then by anyone with whom you wish to share it.

That inner connection is strengthened by spending time in nature, whose healing rhythms bring calm and renewal to our own lives. Nature is not only a great source of external beauty but also a nurturing force that can restore physical and emotional health and beauty, as well.

Actor J. T. Walsh

What's So Special About Being Beautiful?

All of us want to be beautiful, whether we admit it or not. Our desire for beauty is woven into our genes. My ten-year-old-daughter, Rossibel, asks me if she is beautiful, and she is instantly reassured and deeply satisfied when I tell her she truly is. My mother telephoned recently to tell me that someone in her doctor's office couldn't believe she is ninety. The man said she didn't look a day over eighty! She was thrilled by this comment because it made her feel beautiful.

What is this mysterious pull that beauty has on us? Why do beautiful people attract us—or, to put it another way, why do you become such a powerful magnet for people and opportunities when you are beautiful? The reason beauty draws us near is because it arises from love, which is itself the most nourishing and desired force in life. Beauty is the consequence of love, and therefore announces the presence of love, which we are ultimately drawn to.

Making yourself more beautiful is dependent on giving yourself more love. Loving yourself is deeply nourishing and healing. It satisfies you in ways that no other form of love can. When we love ourselves, a mysterious array of chemicals and emotions align, making us physically and emotionally balanced, even radiant. When we love ourselves on a daily basis, our beauty grows very rapidly.

A beautiful woman or man, someone who fundamentally loves herself or himself, exhibits a special type of grace, balance, and integrity that demonstrates for all to see the human potential to be whole.

What Does It Mean to Be Whole?

We hear a great deal about this mysterious state of wholeness that is the basis for health and beauty. What is wholeness, and how can we achieve it? The simplest way to describe it is as a way of living that allows us to love more and more of who we are.

Most of us have been trained to see certain aspects of ourselves in a negative light. We may view our entire physical appearance, or some part of it—our nose or mouth, for example—as unattractive and even ugly. In the same way, we may have been trained to reject aspects of our character as well. Many of us have learned to see our anger, sexuality, power, or desire to perform as negative. Becoming whole is learning to embrace those parts of us that have been rejected or denied and bringing them back into a state of love, compassion, and acceptance. This embrace has a healing effect on our bodies and minds. We become more relaxed inside our skin and more at peace with who we are. When we accept our power as a great gift, we see anger, when used appropriately, as an important self-protective mechanism. When we accept ourselves, we see our sexuality as an essential part of our capacity to love. We give ourselves permission to express abilities and talents that give joy to ourselves and others. We reduce our inner conflicts and tensions. We are no longer divided against ourselves. We are a little more whole, and thus more beautiful.

The beauty that is inside us is expressed in the urge to place flowers on a table, for example, to light a candle at dinner, to harmonize the colors and fabrics of our clothing, to cut and groom our hair in a certain way, to wear cosmetics and use skin care products; even to change our eating habits—all so that we can experience this wondrous aspect of our being. At our Dr. Hauschka offices, we often begin a meeting with a poem or a short philosophical passage that puts us in touch with the beauty that is inside each of us. Not only are we more creative in such an atmosphere, but we are more understanding, open, and supportive of one another, as well. Beauty is healing—and healing leads to greater beauty.

Practicing Beauty

Each chapter in *Awakening Beauty* will provide you with the necessary tools to achieve wholeness and ultimate beauty. After reading about these tools, you will apply them in a twelve-step beauty regimen (provided in chapter 7). This regimen, when practiced for thirty days, will help transform your life. The program provides specific guidance for healing your skin and restoring its youthful, healthy glow. It offers a nonrestrictive healing dietary plan that anyone can follow without experiencing hunger or feeling deprived of favorite foods. It shows you how to gain greater inner peace and emotional balance—not through a regimen of enforced disciplined behaviors but rather by caring for yourself in loving and compassionate ways. This, along with regular exercise, adequate sleep, alleviation of stress, and listening to your body's internal rhythms, provides for a healthier lifestyle, which in turn helps your skin's natural beauty to shine forth.

Dr. Hauschka Skin Care relies on unique hands-on processing methods to capture the therapeutic qualities of healing plants.

Chapter 1

Restoring Beauty
with Rhythm

One of the most powerful ways to establish peace in your life and restore your beauty is to live in harmony with your inner rhythms. Inside you is an internal clock whose pulsations determine when you should wake up in the morning, when you should eat, when your energy levels are peaking, and when it's time for you to rest. These rhythms determine the ebbs and flows of your life.

Most of us live by rhythms that are not our own. Our daily schedules are shaped by the demands of our environment, whether they come from the people we love, our work, or everyday life. Consequently, each day can seem like a psychic tug of war between our own rhythms and those of others. Many of us come to believe that our desires cannot be met unless we have major changes in our lives, like altering important relationships or leaving our jobs. Meanwhile, we go on postponing the inner cry for help and care, which causes us to lose contact with our hearts and age prematurely and, ultimately, causes our beauty to dry up and wither away.

The beauty of your internal rhythmic clock is that it's always there and can always be returned to. No matter how demanding and chaotic your days are, you can still come home to the deeply nurturing beats that are your real life. By practicing listening to and, as much as possible, living by your own inner rhythms, you can find the beauty that is waiting to be discovered.

Your internal rhythms are real—as real as your heartbeat, the rise and fall of your breathing, and the ebb and flow of your hormones. In fact, all biological functions occur rhythmically.

Out of your unique biological cycles come your energy patterns and moods. These waves determine when you are at your best and when you need rest and

recovery. There are periods in your day, week, and month when you have the energy to give, to love, and to nourish others, just as there are periods when your inner rhythms urge you to rest and engage in self-care.

Rhythm is so subtle, yet all-pervasive, that we can easily overlook it. Nature, with her cycles of light and darkness, warmth and cold, stillness and movement, is our biological source and our most immediate example of rhythm.

Each of us uses rhythm to create some degree of order and stability in our lives. You wake up at a certain hour, eat a meal, go to work or perform certain activities at specific hours, come home again at night, and finally fall asleep, only to wake up each morning relatively renewed. Rhythm is the basis for order, and order is the basis for stability, predictability, and good health. Thus, rhythm is an antidote to our fear of the unexpected.

We are beings in search of the deep rhythms of our inner lives. The more we listen to our inner music and act in accordance with it, the more we engage in behaviors that nourish us, promote our health, and restore our beauty.

The Warning Signs That You Are Living Against Your Rhythms

Somehow in recent years, serving others—at home with friends and at our jobs—even when it means exhausting ourselves, has become the basis for "being a good person." In doing this, we refuse to acknowledge our physical and psychological need for balance. Our bodies and minds need both rest and a certain amount of care and play to be healthy and happy. When we sacrifice too much, we become exhausted, angry, and fearful. Most of us don't realize this until we are utterly spent, miserable, and in jeopardy of losing our health.

Whenever you are exhausted but give more than is healthy for you, or simply more than you have, your inner world sends out warning signals that appear as either fear or anger or both. Your inner guidance system is telling you to slow down, to back away from life's demands, to rest and recover your connection to yourself.

People who are chronically angry often fail to realize that their inner guidance systems are telling them to come back to themselves and start meeting their own needs. Too much of these angry and fearful emotions can poison our health and strip us of our beauty. These people's inner wisdom is pleading with them: "Pay attention! You need rest. You need time to be alone and time to be with those you love and who love you. You need to have fun, to dance in the sun and walk in the rain. Fill up again. You're empty!"

Therapists working with people who have suffered from substance abuse have coined the acronym HALT—hungry, angry, lonely, tired—to help people recognize the cues that make us vulnerable to self-destructive behaviors. The more time you spend in communion with your own rhythms, the less isolated you will feel—and the more power you have to diffuse the HALT emotions.

As powerful as anger and fear can be, many of us fail to respect them as early warnings of depletion and exhaustion. When we don't listen to these early signals, stronger messages are needed. One of the gentler ways our inner nature forces us to slow down is by allowing us to contract the common cold. Lying on our back, we have no choice but to reconnect with our inner rhythms. We know, if only intuitively, that those rhythms are the source of healing and health. We must relax and give in to the gentle embrace of those rhythms until our body has fully recovered.

Rather than being seen as a reason to reconnect to our need for rest and self-care, the common cold is widely interpreted as a nuisance, something to be conquered with drugs. The pharmaceutical industry has convinced us that rather than listen to our inner rhythms and respond appropriately, we should take a pill or a potion and deny our need for rest and recovery. This is just one of many ways in which modern life steers us away from our innate desire for self-love.

Drifting too far from one's inner rhythms can be dangerous. Even before catastrophe strikes, we suffer a host of losses. We age rapidly and become tired, angry, and fearful, all of which rob us of our beauty. For those who deny the subtle warnings, more extreme measures can arise, such as accidents or illness. How many times have we heard of people who were pushing themselves too hard and then experienced a breakdown in a relationship or got into a car accident because they failed to pay attention? Or of friends who experienced so much stress they became seriously ill or had a heart attack.

Your rhythms support your life and cause it to unfold. By understanding and knowing your rhythms, you develop your sense of self, an ever-increasing capacity for genuine love, and an ever-unfolding beauty.

Discovering Your Rhythms Is Easier Than You May Think

Your beauty, your health, and much of your youthful vitality can be recovered simply by listening to, and returning to, the gentle waves of your inner world that is alive with feelings and thoughts. When we integrate our emotions, thoughts, and actions, we live in harmony with our rhythms. Granted, it's impossible to do this all the time, but the more we bring harmony to our inner lives and outer behaviors, the greater our health and beauty will become.

The first step in this process is simply to experience our own subtle inner feelings. There are many ways to do this. One of the easier ways, for me, is simply to sit in the sun with my cat in my lap. Lucy's deep restfulness is contagious. Her meditative state passes to me. My body relaxes as I look out my window onto my garden and the tall trees that surround my house. Doing "nothing," especially when you do it in the sun or by a window on a rainy day, is a beautiful and much-needed experience.

above Pets' restful, meditative state can be contagious.

As I sit in my garden, the demands of my life retreat. My inner being seems to connect with the natural outside world. In the stillness, I feel the life of the trees, bushes, and flowers rise to meet me. I feel my own life rise in return. Something deep, serene, and beautiful stirs inside me and spreads through my inner world. My breath becomes deeper and more rhythmic. The tension in my lower back, pelvis, and legs releases, and my breath flows deeply into my body. Soon my heart opens and I feel at peace with my world. Time has stopped. My body is deeply relaxed, and I feel whole and happy. I am being healed and nourished in ways that nothing else in my life can provide.

Another simple way to experience your inner rhythms and to bring order to them is to create order in your environment. Often when I feel my life is getting out of control, I organize my office, clean a room in my house, or arrange a drawer or my jewelry box. It sounds mundane, but the act of creating order around me puts me in touch with the order within me. It also helps me avoid trying to control everyone else around me.

Much of life is chaotic, nonsensical, and draining. Rhythm awareness and inner wisdom create a sense of order and peace to combat these negative circumstances. Beauty is your birthright. You will always have the potential to be beautiful as long as you act in harmony with your rhythms.

Practicing Healing Beauty

Your face and body reflect your physical and emotional health. You carry stresses, fears, and anger that alter your inner life and affect your health, happiness, and physical appearance. If you are to be truly beautiful and fulfilled, you must be actively engaged in healing your inner conflicts.

Healing is very different from curing, just as the work of healers is very different from that of medical doctors. *Healing* is the act of ridding the body of the conditions that create and support disease. Most of the illnesses people suffer from today arise primarily from lifestyle-related causes, such as stress, diet, and lack of exercise. Changes in these areas can eliminate many illnesses.

below Time spent in nature can get us back into a healthy rhythm.

Ridding the body of the underlying causes of disease, while at the same time promoting good health, is the act of healing. Healing requires your active participation. As you engage in healing behaviors—exercising more, taking more time for yourself, eating a more healthful diet—you are changed for the better. In anthroposophy, your efforts to promote good health and a better life are known as *salutogenesis,* a word that is derived from the Latin *salus,* meaning health, and the Greek *genesis,* meaning origin. In the next few chapters, I will show you how to use salutogenesis to promote the health and beauty of your skin.

The healing approach to health care is unlike what medical doctors do today. When a doctor tries to cure you of an illness, he or she focuses mainly on the symptoms of your disease. The belief is that when the symptoms are eliminated, the disease has been effectively treated. Drugs are often used to suppress the symptoms, but often the underlying causes of the disease remain in place, which means that stronger and more numerous medications are needed to eliminate its symptoms.

left A warm bath is relaxing and soothing and reconnects us to our personal rhythms.

In most cases, healing and curing can be administered in combination to effectively treat disease. But in order to truly eliminate an illness or any condition that causes you distress, healing is always necessary, especially since most drugs do not address the underlying causes of your problems. There are real-life reasons for your anger, fear, or chronic stress. All of us attempt to repress painful memories. But when we allow certain painful emotions or memories back into our consciousness through the act of self-healing, we are able to welcome them back with acceptance and love, thus becoming more whole. This results in deeper inner peace and tranquillity. You have the strength and resources to confront these problems. But before you can effectively address the challenges you face, you need two forms of support you may not yet have. The first is a compassionate relationship with yourself, achieved by responding to your rhythms and emotions. The second is a healer to help you find these rhythms and, eventually, your authentic beauty.

To find a nonjudgmental healer who is right for you, start by asking friends if they know of a massage therapist or a Reiki practitioner. If your friends don't know anyone, explore day spas in your community that offer massage or other forms of healing touch. You can also ask your doctor, or simply choose someone from the telephone book or local newspaper. You may also want to find out if there is a local school for massage, shiatsu, acupressure, acupuncture, or some other form of therapeutic touch in your area. These types of schools are always looking for volunteers on whom their students can practice and learn their trade. Volunteers usually get a full body treatment for a fraction of the regular cost.

Be clear about the kind of person you are looking for. Will you be more comfortable with a woman or a man? How old should the person be? Remember: The most important characteristics are that she or he be free of judgment and possess a healing manner and touch. Once you find a healer, go regularly.

Use Rhythm to Reinforce Your Healing Practice

It's all well and good to have a massage, acupuncture, or holistic skin care treatment, but one session will not create any lasting effect. The reason is that the impact of the treatment will dissipate with time. In order for gentle forms of therapy such as healing touch, massage, or acupuncture to transform you, their effects must be reinforced with regular treatments. If you want to maximize the power of those treatments, use rhythm to reinforce their healing effects.

Let's say you see a practitioner weekly, or even once a month. Schedule your appointments for the same day each week, or each month, at the same hour—for example, 3 P.M. every Thursday, or 3 P.M. on the third Thursday of each month. Your body, mind, and spirit will then become aware that they are getting a boost of healing energy in a rhythmic, or wavelike, pattern. With continued treatments, that pattern will be reinforced, deepened, and strengthened. Soon, your internal rhythms will rise automatically as the time approaches for your treatment, thus boosting your self-healing forces and conditioning your body to heal. That healing will show in your skin, your face, and your body.

A series of healing baths puts you in touch with your inner life and, at the same time, helps heal the imbalances that may be causing distress. Make a ritual of this practice and see if it doesn't also stir feelings of deep inner peace.

Once you have had your bath, rested, and written in your diary, try doing a simple exercise created by Rudolf Steiner to speed healing and spiritual development. Remember the day's details in reverse order—that is, start recalling your day from the evening to afternoon to morning to dawn. Steiner maintained that by doing this exercise, we digest and integrate the events, emotions, and insights of the day. In effect, we get more out of the day and, by extension, our lives. We also deepen the lessons learned that day, which makes them more useful and available to us as we go through life. The exercise sounds simple, but it takes practice. Do it while sitting in a chair. Usually, you'll get sleepy long before you

awakening beauty

20

have fully reviewed the events that took place that day. That's fine. It's a good way to allow yourself to get tired and prepare for sleep.

As you practice this exercise, you'll increasingly see yourself in a more objective light because you'll witness yourself from an outside perspective, discovering things about your behavior you never saw before. For example, many people see the ways in which they unconsciously block effective communication, or how they fail to notice the love someone is trying to give them. As you witness yourself struggling to deal with some issue, you also awaken your compassion for yourself, which is extremely healing.

Baths to Cleanse the Soul

One of my favorite rhythmic practices is to take a series of healing and restorative baths. I choose a particular night each week, say Wednesday, and a particular hour, say 8 P.M., and maintain this rhythm for seven weeks. After the bath, I rest for about twenty minutes, or as long as I was in the bath, and then write in my diary for another half hour to an hour. This healing practice can be enhanced by adding essential oil concentrates to each bath. I choose an essential oil to balance my temperament or mood at the time, or one that is appropriate to the season.

The philosophical movement of anthroposophy maintains that very small quantities of a medicinal substance could be charged with energy and thus made more powerful by shaking or stirring the medicine repeatedly. This practice, which originated with homeopathy, came to be known as *potentization* or *succussion*. The sudden shaking—succussion—charges the medicine with a jolt of energy that catalyzes the medicine and makes it more potent.

You can give your bath greater healing potential by gently circulating the water in the shape of a figure 8 until vortexes appear in the water. As you circulate the water, notice the change in the feeling and texture of the water as you potentize it. The water feels more silky, homogeneous, and slightly more viscous. It's as if the water suddenly became more integrated and powerful.

In nature, pure, clean water is always moving in rhythmical patterns, as within a river or a brook. You can bring this same healing approach to your own bathing rituals. Masaru Emoto, a renowned Japanese scientist and author of the book *The Hidden Messages in Water*, discovered that water is highly sensitive to words, vibrations, and even thoughts. Emoto found that words have different effects on water depending on their meaning, and showed that when water is quickly frozen into crystals after it is exposed to life-supporting words such as *love* and *gratitude*, the crystals are stunning in their beauty and order.

Here are five types of essential oils that can be used in a healing bath cycle to cleanse and harmonize your spirit.

Lavender Oil

Lavender relaxes muscles and calms and soothes the nervous system. Any time you are under stress or on the edge of anger or fear, take a lavender bath to bring you back into balance and harmony. Lavender cools hot skin conditions such as inflamed capillaries and rashes. It relaxes and moistens dry skin, soothes nerves, and reduces redness and itching. Because it cools, lavender is great for hot summer nights. It is a perfect evening bath.

Lemon Oil

Essential oil of lemon refreshes and restores us when we suffer from physical exhaustion. Used as a healing tonic in virtually every culture, fresh-squeezed lemon or its essential oil refreshes and tones the skin, restoring its youthful glow. Lemon juice or lemon oil is also used as an astringent to close oozing skin or treat rashes and allergies that cause too much moisture in the skin and sinuses. Lemon is an ideal bath for spring and summer.

Rosemary Oil

Rosemary promotes circulation. It warms, rejuvenates, and relaxes the body. Take a rosemary bath if you have chronically cold hands and feet or when you just can't get warm. Rosemary also strengthens and warms the spirit. It is traditionally used when we feel weak, shy, or afraid, or suffer from figurative cold feet and simply can't face the world. Rosemary helps us relax when we've been working too hard for too long or feel overwhelmed by our problems. Rosemary is also used to treat sallow, listless skin because it brightens and restores color. All of this makes rosemary ideal for a fall and winter series of baths. Because it is so energizing, it's also a wonderful way to begin the day.

Sage Oil

Spruce Oil

Sage is used traditionally as a smudge to cleanse the spirit before sacred rituals. A sage bath neutralizes hostile or negative thoughts and emotions, drawing out anger, fear, and sadness from the tissues. It soothes and cleanses the internal rhythms of heavy or dark emotions and thoughts. A sage bath also can be used to treat body acne.

Spruce reins in emotions that seem out of control. It soothes and opens the lungs and the entire rhythmic system, restoring us when we feel emotionally exhausted, spent, and burned out. Spruce is an ideal bath for late winter and early spring, as well as whenever your lungs or sinuses are congested.

Healing Is As Simple As a Walk in the Park

Here's a simple prescription to reduce stress and fear and to restore sanity: Walk in a park or be in nature at least once a week. The healing becomes stronger when you take the nature cure more often. Nature's loving rhythms and healing energies are still the most rejuvenating forces. A few days at the ocean or in a cabin by a lake brings us back to our senses. A walk in the mountains or some time by a river awakens the subtle cadences of our inner world, restoring the beauty within. After a few days in nature's rhythmic embrace, you will begin to feel tension melt away, allowing the subtle energies within you to surface. In no time, your physical and emotional health is rejuvenated and your beauty restored.

Take nature's cure today by choosing a day each week to eat lunch in the park or spend twenty minutes or more walking amid the trees with a friend—or alone. Notice the trees in every season. Look at the flowers as they are gently shaken by the wind and seem to dance and call out for your attention. Take the colors of nature into your spirit so that they enrich and transform your inner life. Breathe deeply and exhale the tension from your body and mind. Feel your inner rhythms rise in the presence of such beauty.

Exercise for Rhythm, Not for Fitness

When we think of exercise, most of us think of pain. We have been trained to think of some idealized state of fitness as the goal toward which we should strive. However, understanding your body's rhythm changes can change your approach to exercise. Your new goal is to come into harmony with your internal environment; this will dramatically reduce your stress levels, give you a deep experience of peace, and restore your sense of self, allowing you to think more clearly. As a result, you will have a healthier perspective on the circumstances of your life and make smarter decisions.

With rhythm as your goal, walk with the intention of harmonizing your speed and distance with how you feel inside. Today you may be in a reflective mood. If so, walk slowly and allow yourself to feel and think deeply. You may be in that reflective state for a week or many weeks. Walk to support your reflective state of mind. If tomorrow you feel light and joyful, walk lightly and joyfully. Next week, you may be full of energy. Perhaps you will want to walk at a faster pace. You may even want to run for a distance. Go for it. But when your body says "Slow down or rest," listen to it. And when your body says, "Let's start up again," do so. Practice moving according to your inner guidance.

Both rhythm and exercise function as waves. The rising part of the wave is when energy is being expended in ever-greater quantities until the expenditure reaches its peak. The declining part of the wave is when energy is being burned more slowly until you reach a point of rest. During the burn phase, muscles are working hard and tissues are breaking down. During the resting phase, you are gathering energy, healing the body, and rebuilding tissues. We see this wave pattern clearly when we consider the effects of exercise on our muscles and bones. During the workout phase, muscle and bone tissue are stressed and broken down. During the recovery phase, muscle and bone are healed and rebuilt; in many cases, both become stronger than they were before we exercised.

Exercise is a threefold phenomenon: energy expenditure rises; energy expenditure slows; rest occurs, and energy recovery takes place. By engaging consciously in each aspect of the rhythmic nature of exercise, we promote the body's ability to heal, rebuild, and recover. Therefore, when you walk, or do any exercise, remain conscious of your inner rhythms. The speed and distance you walk should reflect your inner world, not a fantasy image of fitness. Expend the energy that your body can give up. Give your body as much rest as it needs to fully recover.

In this way, you can make walking a meditation—light and happy sometimes, contemplative and reflective at others, angry and full of turmoil occasionally. Let your rhythms guide your exercise patterns.

You might also want to consider doing other activities that expand your connection to your internal rhythms. Eurythmy, which means beautiful, harmonious movement, is a new art form; inspired by Rudolf Steiner, it is both a dancelike and a therapeutic exercise. It is designed to foster an intimate connection among body, emotions, and spirit through expanding and contracting movements. It is taught at Waldorf Schools—the schools inspired by Steiner to develop the whole child—and any anthroposophical foundation in your local community. Yoga, which means union of body, mind, and spirit, is an exercise designed to put you in touch with your inner rhythms. Tai chi chuan, which means the harmonious movement of the life force, or chi, is a martial art based on rhythmic movements. It is a meditative dance whose purpose is to attune you to your own internal waves and energies. Other martial arts can do the same, as long as the movement is a direct reflection of your own internal rhythms.

The added benefit of the rhythmic approach to exercise is that it actually results in fitness and improved health. Even small amounts of exercise, especially walking, dramatically improve healing. A study done by Harvard researchers and published in the March 2001 issue of the *Journal of the American Medical Association* showed that women who walk just one hour a week have half the risk of heart disease and heart attack as those who are sedentary. Other research has shown that regular, moderate walking reduces the risk of heart disease, cancer, diabetes, and high blood pressure in both men and women. Regular walking dramatically reduces a woman's risk of breast cancer. The point is to move—walk, dance, or perform some other activity. Do it for the pleasure, not the perfection.

Yoga is an exercise based on your inner rhythms.

Zen Exercise:
Do Nothing and Gain the Entire World

In addition to physical exercise, schedule at least twenty minutes each week in which your only activity is to sit comfortably in your home, or in your garden, and feel your feelings.

There are some rules for this activity, however. First, you cannot go to sleep. Second, you cannot watch television, write, or do any other activity. Third, if you find that you are in a highly emotional state, allow your emotions to emerge into clarity until you feel compassion for yourself. Once you achieve this, your inner world will be clear, and the love and healing energies will flow.

At the very least, this is a time of profound rest and deep healing. But this practice also reveals all types of inspiration and guidance from deep within you. Many things become clear. If you are struggling with a major decision, the answer will come to you. By doing nothing, you allow the subtle wisdom within you to rise and guide you. Along with inspiration will come clarity, enthusiasm, and the courage to follow the path before you.

A Meditative Ritual at the Start of
Your Day and Before Each Meal

One of the most powerful antidotes to chaos and fear is the restoration of a union with ourselves through meditation. Any form of meditation or reflective contemplation will work if you make a direct and personal connection to the practice. You may recite a prayer you learned in childhood or engage in a ritual or meditation you learned as an adult. The idea is to direct your mind to a particular image or set of words that uplifts you.

There need not be any prescribed time limit, either. Meditation can take as little as five minutes or much longer, if you prefer. But try to do it every morning at the same time and preferably in the same place whenever possible. If you feel it is appropriate, make a simple altar in a peaceful part of your home, or conduct your practice in your garden, under a great tree, or in a private meadow.

By engaging in a meditative or ritual act at the same time each morning, you add to your internal rhythm, which gives your prayer a powerful humility and a simple beauty. At the same time, you are training your body, mind, and spirit to open up at the same hour each day to the mystery and power that

Here are a few universal prayers and meditations you can use each morning as a start to your practice.

Waking up this morning, I smile,
Twenty-four brand-new hours
   are before me.
I vow to live fully in each
   moment
And to look at all beings with
   eyes of Compassion.

—A prayer by Thich Nhat Hanh

Surrender to nature's beauty; I
   find myself in her
The beauty of the world
   strengthens and empowers me
Beauty unites spirit with my
   being
I bear summer in me like a seed

—From *The Calendar of the Soul*
   by Rudolf Steiner, translated by
   Christopher Bamford

Beauty behind me,
Beauty all around me,
Above me and below me hovers
   the beautiful.
I'm surrounded by beauty; I am
   immersed in it.
In my youth, I am aware of it,
And in old age, I shall walk
   quietly the beautiful path.
In beauty it is begun. In beauty it
   is ended.

—Navaho prayer

underlies the entire universe. When done consistently, this act becomes the foundation of your day and, eventually, your life. Your practice becomes the spiritual haven to which you retreat in times of difficulty, the place where you go to give thanks for all that you have been given.

Many people prefer to pray or meditate in movement, such as sacred dance, yoga, or a martial art such as tai chi chuan. If any one of these practices gives you the experience of connection and faith, then by all means engage in it daily.

If you like, you can make a small expression of thanks before each meal as well. In our house, we light a candle at dinner each night and say a prayer in which we thank the sun and the earth for our food. This small ritual allows us to relax and prepares our body to receive food. It also reminds us to be grateful for what we have been given. You can do this unobtrusively, without calling attention to yourself. Simply bow your head, close your eyes, and take a moment to be aware of your gratitude.

The Four Faces Within

Choosing the bath, exercise, or meditative practice that's right for you depends on your ability to see your current imbalances. One of the most effective tools for self-examination and rebalancing is the Four Temperaments.

The Four Temperaments is a typology, or ancient form of psychology, for understanding the four different personality types. Created by the ancient Greeks, who associated each personality type with an aspect of nature, the Four Temperaments has been studied throughout history and refined by leading psychologists and philosophers, including the twentieth-century philosopher and scientist Rudolf Steiner.

Each of the four personality types has a positive and a negative pole. Each type can become imbalanced and turn into its own source of stress and conflict. At that point, we need to figure out how the imbalance arose and what we can do to right the ship again and regain our rhythm and balance.

It's important to keep in mind that we all possess these four temperaments. We tend to be more comfortable with one or two of them, but all four are within us. The more we explore each temperament, the more we can navigate in and out of each one, depending on the demands of the situation we are facing. That is a kind of mastery that each of us is striving for. The more wedded we are to a single temperament, the more likely we are to suffer the imbalances associated with that way of being.

Choleric Temperament: Let's Get It Done—Now!

When you are in the choleric temperament, you are a doer and a leader. You take on challenges and get things done. You're active and focused on your work. You meet deadlines; you complete tasks. During such periods, you often have great stamina, lots of energy, and determination. You're resolute. You tend to forget your personal concerns and concentrate instead on the details of the job or challenge facing you. Hence, significant accomplishments are possible.

Physically, you radiate confidence and power. There's a certain authority in your walk and presence. You're grounded, practical, and sure of yourself. All of this shows in your appearance.

The ancient Greeks associated this temperament with the fire element—and, indeed, when you are in the choleric temperament, your emotions tend to be fiery. But as stress builds, your determination can turn into stubbornness. Your attention to detail and insistence on making things right can become the basis for frustration and outbursts of anger. You can also become excessively controlling, which leads to more frustration fear, and anger. In the extreme, you can forget the sensitivities of others and can easily offend. As the imbalance becomes more acute, you can bring the job home with you and become excessively demanding and intolerant of those you love. Conflicts arise at work and at home. Just as your temperament becomes hotter, your face becomes increasingly inflamed, flushed, hot, and red. Your need to relax can easily lead you to indulge in excesses of sweets, alcohol, or television, which can actually feed the tension and result in more conflict.

Whenever an imbalanced choleric nature arises, it's time to relax, back up, and exhale. There's more to life than work and accomplishment. Besides, an imbalanced choleric temperament tends to waste a lot of energy in emotion and flare-ups. You become an impediment to your progress rather than a catalyst for forward movement. In the end, a person whose choleric nature takes over gets less done than do people who are able to relax and stay focused on the task at hand.

When you find your choleric temperament out of control, take a warm lavender bath. Lavender cools and relaxes the body. It reduces tension and inflammation. As the tension dissipates, circulation improves. Soon you will find your emotional life softening and your perspective opening up. New and creative solutions will emerge.

In addition to the lavender bath, take a gentle walk at lunchtime as well as after work. Don't power walk—always the symptom of an imbalanced choleric—but stroll. Spend time in nature, feeling its nourishing rhythms and returning to the stillness inside you. Get a massage, listen to soft music, and talk about your inner conflicts and frustrations with someone who loves and supports you.

Meanwhile, increase your consumption of cooked vegetables, avoid spicy foods, and reduce or eliminate alcohol. Soon you'll be back in balance, enjoying all the positive aspects of the choleric nature.

Sanguine Temperament: All Is Groovy

The sanguine temperament is characterized by optimism, humor, and a generally upbeat nature. You're positive, happy, and bent on enjoying life. Little or nothing gets you down. There's a spring in your step and a song in your heart. You tend to say just the right thing at the right moment. You've got plenty of emotional surplus, which makes you generous, understanding, and tolerant. At a party, you are the bon vivant.

All of this can have an extremely positive effect on your appearance. In the sanguine temperament, you often glow. Your attractiveness is at an all-time high. You are your most beautiful self. Your movements tend to be light and graceful, your words gentle and witty. What people see on the outside is what you are experiencing on the inside. How could there be a downside to this beautiful temperament?

Sanguines can actually carry the good life a little too far, partly due to intense curiosity. You want to study everything. Life thoroughly fascinates you, and every subject seems to draw your attention. Consequently, it's hard to focus and stay grounded. It's as if life has given you wings and all you can do is fly from one subject to the next, like a bee pollinating flowers. The more the sanguine nature becomes imbalanced, the less committed you are to any single endeavor or any individual person. You have trouble getting things done. You can't concentrate, discipline yourself, or work hard. You become impractical, flighty, and—like the element with which this temperament is associated—a little too airy. You party too much, work too little, and make mistakes too easily. There's little depth in your emotional life and virtually no real understanding of life's real demands.

When the sanguine pole is out of balance, it's time to get real. The place to start is with a spruce bath. Spruce has a dense, resinous aroma that grounds the senses and restores our intimate connection with our body and nervous system. Spruce strengthens our roots, our connection to the earth. It keeps our feet on the ground. It awakens and restores our practical nature.

In addition to the spruce bath, try vigorous physical exercise. Walk daily, putting a little vim and vigor in your step. Feel your body. Breathe deeply and exhale. Come back to yourself and your senses. Get a massage. Let a skilled healer put you back in touch with your body.

Eat more cooked whole grains, such as brown rice, millet, and barley. Whole grains strengthen the nervous system and ground us. This is a good time to eat high-quality, biodynamic animal foods, such as fish, eggs, turkey, or chicken, all of which can put us back in touch with our power and help ground us on the earth. Avoid sugar, alcohol, and (needless to say) recreational drugs.

The Phlegmatic: Everything's in Order, and I Want to Keep It That Way!

The phlegmatic temperament gives you the ability to think things through, to envision the future, and to create a plan for the fulfillment of your goals. This is the part of you that loves order and finds safety in routine. Your phlegmatic character creates rhythm, consistency, and stability. It loves the predictable. When you're in this character type, you are stocking up for the winter and making sure the car is tuned up and the oil's been changed. You balance the books; you're careful with your resources; you're frugal. You want tranquillity. Consistency is happiness. Thus, you guard against the unexpected as if it were a thief in the night. You don't like ups and downs. You are wise, temperate, and cautious. You tend to keep life and all of its gadgetry simple. You're patient. You don't need quick results—in fact, you're suspicious of anything that makes big promises or offers overnight rewards. You're meditative and appreciative of subtle pleasures. You like the tried and true. Nothing fancy, please. People can count on you.

As wonderful as all of these qualities are, when you're out of balance they can form a kind of prison. Life becomes ponderous, predictable, and flat with no excitement and little joy. You can become dull and boring to the point where the routine seems to choke the life out of you. Nothing seems important nor particularly valuable. Life comes and goes. Even more insidious, you can get so wedded to your routine that you become paralyzed. Your stubborn attachment to routine can actually be a cover for a fear of anything that is new, exciting, or unpredictable.

In other words, it's time to wake up. A lemon bath provides a therapeutic awakening of the nervous system and the senses. Lemon captures the warmth and energy of the sun. It pierces and disperses the dense clouds of stagnation that occur when the phlegmatic is stuck in his or her routine. It lightens the mood and brings freshness and energy to a lethargic life condition.

In addition to the lemon bath, eat more warming spices, such as garlic, cumin, coriander, pepper, and roasted red pepper, all of which warm and awaken the heart. Minimize dairy products, which can reinforce the phlegmatic nature by creating stagnation. Listen to music that inspires you, lifts your spirit, and opens your heart. Let yourself remember old ambitions and dreams. Do something entirely different each day. Dance—ballroom, swing, tango, or rock and roll. Dancing is that rare combination of rhythm and excitement, consistency and aliveness in movement. Take up a new hobby, such as tennis, golf, or billiards. Plan a trip to an exotic location that you've never visited but always wanted to see. In short, break out of your routine.

The Melancholic Temperament: He Ain't Heavy, He's My Brother

When you are in the melancholic nature, you are caring, compassionate, and openhearted. You think about life less from the practical perspective than from the philosophical. You are spiritually oriented. You see the big picture and the great sweep of history. Yet you connect to individuals, especially to their pain. You listen attentively to people who want to share their tale of woe.

In the melancholic pole of your nature, you are introverted and extremely sensitive. You feel your own emotions intensely and can become preoccupied with your own emotional distress. You are often intuitive and highly perceptive about life, people, and people's histories. Your intellect is highly charged. You're often filled with philosophical or psychological insight—yet you are less interested in the future than the past. You want to understand yourself and how you got to where you are today. You struggle to connect the dots. You are preoccupied with the inner world but largely detached—at least in practical ways—from the outer one. You are more involved in your interior life than in changing the bigger world around you.

In the melancholic character, you can be extremely moody, moving from elation to depression within minutes. You also tend to worry a lot, especially about your physical health. When the melancholic nature takes over, you can easily become a hypochondriac. Melancholics wallow in deep existential questions, often finding pleasure in worry and dread. Eventually, the negative thinking associated with this temperament gets the better of you. It can cause physical distress, depression, and a wide array of physical ailments. This occurs largely because your life force has moved up into the head and drained the etheric body of its vital energies, thus causing the physical body to suffer. You become increasingly introverted. As this occurs, you experience less and less of your natural effectiveness and power.

If the melancholic nature has gotten the better of you, it's time to get out of your head and back into your body. Start with a series of rosemary baths, which will warm your body, awaken your senses, and dramatically boost your circulation. Rosemary revitalizes the body and lights the fire of our physical powers and passion. It puts us back in touch with the choleric nature and its inherent tendency to action and adventure. Also, try soaking your feet in spruce bath oils, which will ground you as well.

In addition to the rosemary baths and spruce foot soaks, eat cooked whole grains and root vegetables daily. Avoid raw vegetables and raw fruit, both of which cool the body and send the life forces upward. Keep your body warm, especially your feet (in winter, wear extra socks).

The Four Temperaments is a wonderful tool for self-analysis and self-healing. You can use it to understand your imbalances and to know what you can do to relieve stress and get back in step with your inner rhythms.

Rhythm is one of the great powers available to us if we learn how to experience it and use it for our own benefit. Follow your rhythms all the way to your most authentic and rewarding experience of beauty.

Chapter 2

The Healing Power of Plants

When I am asked to give examples of authentic beauty, I often recall the country women of the Mediterranean region, Asia, and Africa—women who radiate vitality, health, and earthiness. Their skin is so clean and pure. How did they become so beautiful? A big part of the answer is plants. Plants are the source of most of their food, medicine, and skin care. What's more, their plants are pure. They are grown in healthy soil that is largely free of harmful poisons and pesticides. The plants are a rich source of healing substances and vital energies.

This is the essence of the Dr. Hauschka way to authentic beauty. Heal the soil so that it produces the most powerful healing and medicinal plants. These life-giving plants are the basis for your diet and skin care—and thus your beauty. Live as much as possible by your own rhythms and spirit. The alchemy that results from this simple formula will transform you. Good health and true beauty will be yours.

Our society has moved away from pure, nonpolluted plants as the primary source of nutrition and skin care. Our food is often highly processed and high in calories, fat, and synthetic additives. It is grown in soil that is largely devoid of humus, the living matter in topsoil that makes agriculture possible. In place of humus, we have petrochemical fertilizers, herbicides, and pesticides, many of which were originally made from the unused bombs of World Wars I and II. Scientists now tell us that some of these substances cause disease and premature death.

Our animals are no better off. Most of them are injected with hormones and antibiotics, traces of which turn up in our food and affect the hormones and overall health of both children and adults. The hormones alone are believed to affect the growth and development of children. Many scientists now believe these same food-based steroids also play a role in the proliferation of breast, ovarian, and prostate cancers.

This same synthetic approach is applied to most skin care products. Most of us are applying a collection of chemicals and petroleum products to our faces. These may confer a small, short-term benefit, but they actually have long-term consequences. Many people are sensitive to these synthetic chemicals, and others are allergic to them. Rather than stem the aging process, some of these chemicals accelerate it. For example, parabens, the most widely used preservatives in skin care and cosmetics products, have a hormonelike effect on the skin and trigger inflammation, causing heat and swelling inside the tissues of your face. Inflammation shrinks the collagen fibers, the strands of protein that make your skin elastic, resulting in wrinkling and more rapid aging.

The effects of our modern farming, diet, and skin care are devastating. Skin problems abound, including premature aging, discoloration, acne, rosacea, and skin cancers. Obesity, digestive disorders, and a plethora of degenerative diseases are all on the rise.

You have the power to live in a more whole and healthful way. No matter who you are, you can reverse this alarming trend. Health and beauty are your birthright. You can take steps today to improve both. The place to start is with rhythm, as discussed in the previous chapter. The next essential step is to eat high-quality plant foods grown in rich, nonpolluted soil, meaning produce grown by biodynamic or, at the very least, organic methods. This same principle must be applied to your skin care products.

Quality and purity are the most important guidelines in choosing your foods as well as the substances you apply to your face and body. To make full use of these two lifesaving guides, we must understand exactly what they are and why they are so important.

Small-scale farming allows for hands-on care and attention to natural rhythms.

What Does Soil Have to Do with Beauty?

From the soil, health and beauty are born. The soil contains all the vital minerals, such as calcium, magnesium, and iron, that we need to live. But we can't eat the soil, so we've got to have a middleman, so to speak, a medium that supplies us with the earth's nutrients. The middlemen are plants. They absorb nutrients from the earth and make them available to us in the form of delicious foods. The calcium, phosphorus, and other minerals animal foods provide come from plants as well. In addition, plants create other essential substances, such as vitamins, that we need to live and be beautiful. In a great many cases, plants are the only source of substances that are essential for health and beauty.

The quality of the soil determines the quality of the plants grown in it. Soil that is rich in minerals gives rise to mineral-rich plants. Unfortunately, the more poisons in the soil, the more poisons in the plants grown in it and, hence, in the entire food chain.

Soil is a living, breathing life-form. Half a teaspoon of soil contains millions of bacteria and other microscopic organisms. And as every gardener knows, healthy soil also contains lots of worms, which aerate the soil and provide it with oxygen. All of these animals are busy consuming and digesting decayed plants to create a rich black earth called *humus,* which is the principle constituent of topsoil.

Humus contains nutrients, among them nitrogen, phosphorus, and potassium, which are needed to grow plants. Without a nutrient-rich humus, the soil is an infertile desert that cannot grow anything.

At the start of the twentieth century, farmers began adding synthetic fertilizers, pesticides, and herbicides to the soil as a way of creating more abundant crop yields. Unfortunately, these methods depleted the topsoil and

In biodynamic agriculture, soil is regarded as a living, breathing life-form.

What Is Biodynamic Farming?

Biodynamic agriculture is the scientific use of crop rotation, composting, integrated soil, crop and pest management, and animal husbandry pioneered in the early twentieth century. These agricultural practices were later popularized by the organic movement. Both forms of agriculture are ecologically sound and fundamental to the health of the earth, plants, and human beings.

Biodynamic agriculture:

- Applies an organic and sustainable approach to farming that considers not only the health of the ecosystem but also the rhythms of the universe. The sun, moon, planets, and stars influence how the plants grow.

- Applies herbal preparations to the earth to enliven and harmonize plants, compost, and soil.

- Addresses the source of problems rather than the symptoms. A biodynamic farmer looks to the ecosystem to find and correct the imbalance that caused the insect infestation.

began killing the humus. In time, the upper layer of the soil became little more than dust, which was easily carried away by wind and rain.

In 1924, farmers from eastern Germany went to Rudolf Steiner and told him the soil was dying. The humus was so depleted, the farmers said, that it would not be long before they would become dependent on petrochemicals in order to grow food. What could be done?

Farms, Steiner responded, are ecosystems that must be addressed holistically, not only within the farm itself but through its connection to the sun, moon, planets, and stars. He provided a series of healing practices that fell into two broad categories—biological and dynamic. Biological practices banned all synthetic substances, such as artificial pesticides and fertilizers. At the same time, sustainable practices, including the use of green manures, composting, cover crops, crop rotation, and companion planting, were incorporated.

Dynamic practices were intended to increase the life force of the earth in general and the farm in particular. Some of these practices were remedies, or preparations, that were applied to soil, the leaves of plants, and compost piles in order to make the growing plants stronger and healthier. Others required that the farmer stimulate energy patterns in the earth in the same way that an acupuncturist unblocks the flow of energy within the human body and restores its balance. Soon after adopting these practices, farmers began to see the recovery of the topsoil and the rejuvenation of the plants. Both plants and seeds were hardier and more resistant to illness and changing weather patterns. But the farmers noticed something else: the flavor of the food was richer, more delicious.

Out of the biodynamic movement (see sidebar) came organic agriculture. In essence, organic farmers adopted many of the green methods of the biodynamic growers, but they stopped short of the more spiritual aspects of biodynamics, namely, the many biodynamic practices and preparations designed to enhance the life force of the earth and strengthen its connection with cosmic forces.

Biodynamic and organically grown foods are free of all synthetic poisons. Only natural substances, derived directly from the earth, can be used at any stage in the growing and harvesting of organic foods. In the case of animals, organic farmers use no growth hormones and antibiotics. Only organic feed is used, and the animals are allowed to roam and live under humane conditions.

We cannot ingest agricultural toxins and expect to be healthy and beautiful. Every time we consume these substances, they touch off an immune reaction that affects our skin and makes us vulnerable to illness.

How Diet and Agriculture Affect Aging and Beauty

Two underlying processes make us age more rapidly than we need to and are linked to most of today's illnesses, including heart disease, cancer, diabetes, Parkinson's disease, and Alzheimer's disease. They are *inflammation* and *oxidation.*

Inflammation is nothing more than your immune system's reaction to your ingestion of a poison. When your immune system perceives a threatening substance in your diet, or in the air you breathe, or in the water you drink, it mounts a powerful and multipronged attack on the invader. Part of that response is to create inflammation, which we recognize as heat, swelling, and redness. This occurs wherever the immune system is engaged in a battle—in the tissues of your face, in your arteries, and in your vital organs. Inflammation is essential to keeping us alive, but it also causes collateral damage, such as scarring and wrinkling.

The more poisons we are exposed to, the more inflammation our body suffers. All those pesticides and fertilizers we consume, for example, trigger inflammatory responses, which in turn make us age more rapidly.

As your immune cells attack the poisons in your food or the viruses or bacteria you ingest, they create free radicals, or *oxidants.* These highly reactive molecules destroy cells and tissues by causing them to age, form scar tissue, and die.

Free radicals cause all living things to age and decay. They are the reason an apple left on your counter turns brown and shrivels. They make vegetables go bad and milk spoil.

In your skin, free radicals cause the moist collagen fibers that form its superstructure to become dry and shriveled. When the foundation of your skin shrinks, the surface folds over on itself, forming wrinkles. The more free radicals in your system, the more your collagen shrinks and the more wrinkles appear on your skin. Oxidants cause the inside of your arteries to become a landscape of lesions and cholesterol plaques, eventually leading to a heart attack or a stroke. They turn portions of your brain into scar tissue, slowing your thinking and weakening your memory. Eventually, they can cause Parkinson's disease or Alzheimer's disease. They deform the nucleus of cells and trigger the onset of malignancies.

In order to be healthy and beautiful, you must control the amount of inflammation and oxidation in your tissues. One way to do that is to reduce the quantity of poisons you're exposed to, including:

- Alcohol
- Chemical pollutants, including synthetic pesticides, herbicides, fertilizers, petroleum products, and heavy metals
- Cigarette smoke
- Processed foods, including sugar

Healing Plant Substances

The U.S. government and Tufts University have developed a rating system for the antioxidant content of foods. Known as the Oxygen Radical Absorbency Capacity (ORAC) scale, it rates individual foods by their antioxidant powers. The foods are listed here in descending order, beginning with the foods with the highest ORAC ratings, blueberries and blackberries. All the foods listed below are rich sources of antioxidants.

High-Antioxidant (ORAC) Fruits

Blueberries	Oranges
Blackberries	Red grapes
Strawberries	Cherries
Raspberries	Kiwifruit
Plums	

High-Antioxidant Vegetables

Kale	Red bell pepper
Spinach	Onion
Brussels sprouts	Corn
Alfalfa sprouts	Eggplant
Broccoli florets	Collard greens
Beets	

- Saturated fat

- Sunlight

As you can see, the modern diet is an inflammation and free-radical feast, thanks to overprocessing and synthetic additives. So, too, are many so-called skin care products.

We must do more than simply avoid the poisons; we must also give our body what it needs to fight them. That's where antioxidants and other plant substances enter the picture. Antioxidants slow down or stop oxidation, preventing illness and wrinkles. They restore the skin and organs, boost the immune system, promote healing, and slow aging.

There are hundreds and perhaps thousands of antioxidants, though most people have heard of only a few, especially vitamins C and E and beta carotene. In addition, however, most carotenoids—the substances that make vegetables colorful—and phytochemicals act as antioxidants. They are also powerful immune boosters and disease fighters.

Plants:
Where the Antioxidants Are

Plant foods are the only real source of antioxidants, as the following chart shows. The only exception is fish, which provides substantial amounts of vitamin E. All the other animal foods offer either negligible amounts of antioxidants or none at all.

Your beauty and health depend on your daily consumption of plant foods.

AMOUNTS OF VITAMIN C, E, AND BETA CAROTENE

Beta Carotene

No established RDA; scientists recommend between 10 and 30 mg per day

FOOD	SERVING SIZE	AMOUNT/MG	% OF RDA
Brussels sprouts	$1/2$ cup	3.4	11
Carrots	$1/2$ cup	12.2	41
Kale	$1/2$ cup	8.2	27
Mustard greens	$1/2$ cup	7.3	24
Spinach	$1/2$ cup	4.4	15
Squash	$1/2$ cup	16.1	54
Sweet potato	1 med.	2.9	10

Vitamin C

RDA: 60 mg

FOOD	SERVING SIZE	AMOUNT/MG	% OF RDA
Broccoli	$1/2$ cup	49	82
Cabbage	$1/2$ cup	17	28
Cantaloupe	$1/2$ med.	113	188
Cauliflower	$1/2$ cup	34	57
Chile pepper	$1/2$ cup	109	182
Grapefruit	$1/2$ med.	41	68
Green bell pepper	1 med.	95	158
Kale	$1/2$ cup	51	85
Papaya	1 med.	188	313
Potato (baked)	1 med.	26	43
Oranges	1 med.	70	117
Strawberries	1 cup	85	142

Vitamin E

RDA: 10 mg

FOOD	SERVING SIZE	AMOUNT/MG	% OF RDA
Almonds	1 oz.	7.0	70
Apple	1 med.	0.4	4
Asparagus	½ cup	1.8	18
Brown rice	½ cup	1.2	12
Cod	3 oz.	0.8	8
Kidney beans	½ cup	4.4	44
Mackerel	3 oz.	1.5	15
Mango	1 med.	2.7	27
Pinto beans	½ cup	4.1	41
Salmon	3 oz.	1.6–1.8	16–18
Seven-grain bread	1 slice	0.3	3
Shrimp	3 oz.	0.6–3.5	6–35
Sunflower seeds	1 oz.	14.8	148
Sweet potato	1 med.	5.5	55
Wheat	1 cup	0.3	3
Wheat germ	1 cup	20.5	205
Wild rice	½ cup	1.8	18

As the chart reveals, your beauty and health depend on your daily consumption of plant foods—namely vegetables, whole grains, beans, and fruit. The United States Department of Agriculture (USDA) recommends that you eat ten servings of fruits and vegetables per day to get all the antioxidants you need. That gives you an ORAC score of at least 3,000 to 3,500, which the USDA says will slow the aging process and protect you against serious illness. Bruce Ames, Ph.D., a professor of biochemistry and molecular biology at the University of California, Berkeley, and a longtime cancer researcher, says that people who eat fewer than five servings of antioxidant-rich foods each day have twice the risk of developing cancer of those who get five or more servings.

We recommend that you try to get a balanced variety of plant foods each day, including whole grains, roots, leafy greens, seeds, and fruits, and to get in as many of these groups at each meal as possible.

The plant foods and herbal preparations described throughout this book contain many other substances that will heal your skin and organs and promote your health and beauty. Medicinal foods and herbs contain substances that slow the aging process and protect the skin and other tissues from decay.

Plant Substances for Health and Beauty

Certain plant foods contain powerful substances that can be especially healing to your skin. Like antioxidants, these chemicals slow aging, restore your beauty, boost your immune system, and fight disease.

- Flavonoids. Found abundantly in apples, cherries, cranberries, celery, kale, onions, black and green teas, red wine, parsley, soybeans, tomatoes, and thyme, flavonoids cool inflammation, slow and even stop oxidation, and thus protect your skin from aging and wrinkling. Flavonoids boost your immune system as well as suppress tumor growth, prevent blood clots, and kill off cancer cells.

- Indoles. Found in the cruciferous vegetables, such as bok choy, broccoli, Brussels sprouts, cauliflower, cabbage, collard greens, kale, mustard greens, rutabaga, sauerkraut, and turnips, indoles reduce inflammation, act as antioxidants, and offer powerful protection against both breast and prostate cancers. Indoles transform cancer-causing estrogens into their more benign forms, thus helping prevent hormone-related cancers.

- Isoflavones. Found in whole grains, beans, berries, fruits, vegetables, and, most abundantly, in soybeans and soybean products, isoflavones act as antioxidants and keep skin youthful and supple, protect bones from loss of calcium and phosphorus, and lower cholesterol. Perhaps most remarkable of all, isoflavones—especially genistein—block blood vessels from attaching to tumors, preventing them from getting the blood and oxygen they need to survive.

- Saponins. Found in whole grains, soybeans, and soybean products, saponins encourage healing of the skin and other tissues and neutralize cancer-causing enzymes in the intestines, thus helping prevent colon cancer.

- Sterols. Found in a wide variety of vegetables and medicinal plants, sterols have been shown to promote better blood circulation and lower blood cholesterol levels.

The diet provided in chapter 7, along with the recipes and meal plans in chapter 9, includes an abundance of delicious plant and animal foods, lots of flavors and textures, sweet desserts, and high-quality oils. This diet will help you achieve your ideal weight while nourishing you with an abundance of nutrition. At the same time, it will promote good health and lustrous, beautiful skin.

Your beauty and your health depend not just on the content of your diet but also on the purity of the foods you eat. The unfortunate truth is that you can choose all the right vegetables, grains, beans, and fruits, and eat what you believe to be appropriate amounts of animal foods, and still poison yourself every day with chemically treated, pesticide-driven products.

the healing power of plants

What Is a Natural and Organic Food or Product?

Ever since the terms *natural* and *organic* were introduced to the marketplace, they have been a source of controversy. Many attempts have been made to define a natural or organic food or a natural skin care product; most resulted in more confusion than clarity. One of the best definitions to emerge came from an association of German manufacturers of drugs, supplements, cosmetics, and personal care products known as the BDIH. These guidelines, in fact, can be applied by anyone, anywhere, to discern if a food or skin care product can be considered "natural."

Here are the criteria you can use when looking for natural foods and skin care products.

- All raw materials are derived from nature.

- They are grown using organic and biodynamic methods.

- They have undergone only minimal processing.

- They are free of synthetic fragrances, colors, and dyes.

continued opposite

Choosing Foods: Quality First

I don't believe in dieting per se. I believe, fundamentally, that you are designed to be healthy and beautiful. It's in your nature—or, to be more precise, it's in your rhythms. The more you live within your rhythms, the more your inner wisdom will guide you to the right food choices and a diet that will lead to health and beauty.

The following guidelines will speed the recovery of both your health and beauty. The first and most important guide to choosing foods is quality. Quality means purity, to be sure, but it also means sustainability. The highest-quality foods—those produced by biodynamic methods—will not only restore your health and beauty, they will also restore the health and beauty of the earth. When you cannot obtain biodynamic foods, I urge you to choose organically grown foods. Anything short of these two will act as a drag on your health and beauty.

Once you have your quality standards in place, choose unprocessed plant foods as the majority of your daily diet. These include whole grains, fresh vegetables, beans, and fruits. Supplement your plant foods with smaller quantities of low-fat animal products, such as fish, low-fat dairy products, eggs, and low-fat meats. We should eat these foods as the Chinese and Mediterranean peoples do—in small quantities, and often as side dishes. This will provide you with all the protein your body needs. If you feel you need more, add more. Finally, allow yourself a small amount of the processed foods you enjoy as a treat. Do not eat these foods every day, but rather once a week, or two or three times a month. The less the better, especially if you want to lose weight. They should be the exception to your everyday diet.

Processed foods are the greatest source of calories in the food supply today and the primary reason we are suffering from an epidemic of overweight and obesity. Processed foods originate with a natural food, such as wheat, corn, potatoes, or sugar beets. During processing, the water, fiber, and many of the nutrients are removed from the natural foods, thus concentrating an enormous number of calories into a much smaller volume of food. A pound of corn, for example, provides only 390 calories, but a pound of corn chips contains 2,450 calories. A pound of cornflakes gives you 1,770 calories. Good old-fashioned popcorn, without butter, gives you 1,730 calories per pound. Add fat in the form of oil or butter and you get at least 2,270 calories per pound.

Natural foods are low in calories and rich in nutrients. As long as you eat mostly natural foods, your diet will naturally cause you to lose weight if you are overweight, or help you maintain a healthy weight.

How to Lose Weight Easily and Feel Satisfied

If you are concerned about losing weight, try to avoid calorically dense foods. A calorie, of course, is the unit by which we measure the energy content of foods. Lots of calories mean lots of potential energy. But if you don't burn all the calories you eat in your daily activities and exercise routine, the excess calories you consume are stored on your body as fat. Processed foods contain so many calories that you cannot possibly burn all the calories they give you. This means they are converted to fat.

In his book *The Pritikin Principle: The Calorie Density Solution,* Robert Pritikin shows how food manufacturers take a great quantity of natural foods, such as potatoes, and turn them into a small volume of processed foods, such as potato chips, all the while concentrating the calories in those chips. A pound of potatoes, for example, provides about 490 calories, Pritikin points out. But a pound of potato chips provides 2,400 calories. How is that possible? Food manufacturers take a lot of potatoes—far more than you could eat in a single sitting—and boil them, chop them, remove all the fiber and water, and then fry them in fat. The result is a relatively small volume of chips containing most of the calories from the original volume of potatoes, plus the calories picked up from the fat. Thus, a big bag of potatoes turns into a 1-pound bag of potato chips—with 2,400 calories.

The short list below will show you that natural plant foods, such as broccoli, carrots, apples, and oatmeal, contain relatively low amounts of calories. Compare these natural foods to the processed ones on the following list. The difference is huge.

- They contain no petroleum-derived synthetics (parabens, propylene glycol, silicones).

- They underwent exclusively nontoxic processing methods, and no synthetic substances (such as PEGs and sodium laureth sulfate) were used to process the ingredients.

- They have not been treated with any form of radiation at any stage of production.

- All efforts were made to ensure the product contains no genetically modified organisms (GMOs).

- The businesses that produce these substances use ecologically friendly harvesting and processing methods.

- No animals were used to test the product or in its production.

- The company producing the substance uses socially responsible business practices.

- The company uses recyclable and biodegradable packaging.

Unprocessed, Whole Plant Foods	Calories per Pound
Apples	270
Black beans, cooked	600
Brown rice, boiled	500
Kale	130
Oatmeal	280
Pasta	560
Potato, baked	490
Spinach	100
Strawberries	140
Yam, baked	525

© Pritikin Longevity Center, used by permission.

Animal Foods	Calories per Pound
American cheese	1,700
Bacon	2,170
Beef brisket	1,550
Butter	3,250
Cheddar cheese	1,820
Corned beef	1,140
Cream cheese, Philadelphia	990
Ground beef, lean, broiled medium	1,235
Halibut, poached	520
Porterhouse steak	1,390
Salmon, poached	660
Spareribs	1,790
Swiss cheese, regular	1,700
Swiss, Kraft ¹/₃ less fat	1,080

Processed Foods	Calories per Pound
Chocolate chip cookies	2,140
Dietetic cookies	2,180
Entenmann's fat-free cookies	1,510
Oreo cookies	2,200
Fat-free whole-wheat crackers	1,620
Shredded Wheat	1,610
Whole-wheat bread	1,280

Why is this important for your weight? It takes 10 calories to support 1 pound of your body weight. That means that if you currently weigh, say, 160, you must eat a diet that contains at least 1,600 calories each day to maintain that 160 pounds. Let's say you now weigh 150 pounds and want to weigh 130. To do that, you must drop your calorie intake to 1,300 calories a day—virtually impossible on a standard American diet but easy on Mother Nature's diet. If most of your food consists of vegetables, beans, whole grains, and fruits, you're going to have to eat a lot of food before you consume 1,300 calories. Here's why.

A pound of broccoli provides only 130 calories. A pound of zucchini contains only 65 calories. Cauliflower has about 110 calories in a pound. And a pound of red tomatoes is just 95 calories. Vegetables contain lots of fiber and water, both of which fill you up but neither of which contains calories. Most cooked beans provide about 600 calories per pound. Most cooked grains, about 500 calories per pound. But remember, it's unlikely that you can eat a

pound of black beans or a pound of brown rice in one sitting. If you're really hungry, the most you'll be able to eat is about a cup of beans in a single sitting—in other words, less than a quarter of a pound, or fewer than 150 calories. A quarter of a pound of cooked brown rice provides about 120 calories. Your daily quantity of vegetables provides far less. On a diet dominated by plant foods, you'll be able to eat throughout the day and still have no trouble keeping your calorie count at 1,200 to 1,500 calories.

Processed foods are also loaded with synthetic chemicals and very often with the most harmful form of fat, *trans fats,* which can come from partially hydrogenated oils. This synthetic form of fat has been linked to an increased risk of heart disease, cancer, and diabetes.

People who eat processed foods often find themselves experiencing intense food cravings. Many of these cravings are driven by a need for *nutrition,* though the people don't realize the source of their hunger. Instead, they eat more processed foods, which only adds on more calories and further depletes their bodies of nutrients.

Inevitably, people start to crave animal foods in order to feel adequately nourished. Unfortunately, processed foods and high-fat animal products combine to form a duo that's destructive to both health and beauty.

All the guidance, menus, and recipes you need to create a diet for healing your beauty are provided in chapter 7, "Practicing Beauty," and chapter 9, "Menus and Recipes for Healthy and Beautiful Skin."

Almost as important as your choice of foods is how and when you eat each day. As with every other part of our life, it's important to bring rhythm to our eating patterns. Try to establish a healthy routine in which you eat breakfast, lunch, and dinner at the same time each day. When you eat, give thanks and appreciate your food. Don't be distracted by the television or the newspaper, but rather relax, taste your food, and accept it gratefully into your body. Rhythm can help train your body to relax at specific times each day and more fully accept nourishment. Rhythm will enhance the healing effects of your food.

above Valerie is a lawyer and an avid biodynamic gardener from New Jersey.

center Composting enriches the soil with nutrients necessary to grow healthy plants.

below Naturally grown foods are rich in nutrients.

the healing power of plants

Plants That Heal Your Skin and Your Beauty

As we eat foods that restore our health and beauty, we must turn to high-quality skin care products for this same effect. The plants used for these products should be grown bio-dynamically or, at the very least, organically.

Special medicinal plants can work miracles for your skin. They are powerful sources of healing that people have been using to restore beauty for thousands of years. Here are some of the most effective plants for your skin. They can be found in many skin care products and salves. Apply these plant substances to your face and body, and watch your skin be transformed. Chapters 4 and 5 offer recipes for preparing skin care products of your own that include many of these healing and medicinal plants.

Anthyllis *Anthyllis vulneraria L*

(A member of the pea family. Also known as kidney wretch.*)*

Anthyllis produces a yellow to orange flower between April and June. It flourishes in clover fields and unfertilized stretches of land, usually by the side of the road, where only the strongest plants survive. All of this reveals anthyllis's strong life force, or vegetative power, in which traditional healers saw powerful restorative properties.

Anthyllis appears to promote urinary and kidney health. Traditional herbalists in Europe used anthyllis to heal wounds and treat skin disorders of all types, including acne, rosacea, dermatitis, and skin rashes.

Bryophyllum *Kalanchoe daigremontiana*

Family: Crassulaceae

Often referred to as *mother of thousands,* bryophyllum is a succulent water-bearing plant that along its leaves contains dozens of tiny versions of itself, like a mother carrying her young. These shoots fall from the mother plant, become embedded in the earth, and grow independently. Thus, wherever you find one bryophyllum, you're likely to find the rest of its family nearby.

Bryophyllum holds water and thrives in dry climates.

Bryophyllum is an excellent moisturizer. It rejuvenates the skin while stimulating it to retain its own moisture. It also contains many healing chemicals, including calcium and flavonoids. It is highly anti-inflammatory and immune boosting, and promotes wound healing. As it moisturizes, it also heals and restores the skin's flexibility, durability, and firmness.

Calendula (Marigold) *Calendula Officinalis L*

Family: Compositae/ Asteraceae

Calendula, whose beautiful yellow-orange flower blooms between April and June, is one of the most widely used and effective medicinal plants. Ancient healers discovered this remarkable botanical when they recognized that it bloomed each day at approximately 9 A.M. and closed around 3 P.M., with the rising and setting of the sun. This immediately suggested that calendula could absorb and retain the potent healing energies of the sun.

Calendula is loaded with powerful healing substances, including essential oils, saponins, carotenoids, bitter compounds, and flavonoids. It has been used throughout Europe to heal wounds, reduce inflammation, and treat bruises, burns, cuts, and skin ulcers.

Calendula regulates the skin's metabolism and promotes blood circulation. In skin care, it has been used to treat acne, eczema, rosacea, and skin that has been injured or inflamed or irritated.

German Chamomile *Matricaria Recutita*

Family: Compositae

Chamomile is another widely used herb. Its bloom is a little white flower with a yellow center. The flower is the part of the plant used for medicinal purposes. When applied to the skin, chamomile relaxes muscles, connective tissues, and the skin itself. It also relieves muscle spasms. When consumed internally, it relieves anxiety, headaches, nervous tension, and cramps.

Chamomile is an immune booster and is frequently used in tea form to treat cold and flu symptoms. It also enhances liver and digestive function. Chamomile tea combined with two slices of ginger can relieve painful menstrual and digestive cramps. Chamomile is a common herb in skin care products and healing salves, and it is widely available in tea leaf form.

Lavender *Lavendula officinalis, Lavendula augustifolia, Lavendula vera*

Family: Labiatae

Lavender is a woody shrub with beautiful blue and violet flowers that grow upward in tight swirls that look a little like cones. It originated in the Mediterranean region and now is grown in Europe and the United States, among other countries.

Lavender is one of the most effective and widely used herbs in skin care and healing. It is an anti-inflammatory, an antispasmodic, and an antiseptic. You can apply the essential oil directly to the skin, especially over aching or tense muscles, painful spasms, and aching joints. It is deeply relaxing while at the same time uplifting and inspiring. Lavender has a similar effect in baths.

The essential oil of lavender is helpful in treating acne, dermatitis, rosacea, oily skin, and dry skin. It balances the skin and stimulates cellular renewal and healing. In aromatherapy, lavender relaxes and soothes the troubled heart and mind.

the healing power of plants

Lemon *Citrus limon L*

Family: Rutaceae

Lemon is the fruit of a tree that can grow to 15 feet in height. It is one of the most widely used culinary fruits in the world. In Chinese medicine, lemon is used in small amounts, with water, to cleanse and heal the liver and promote digestion and stronger bowel elimination. Rudolf Steiner used lemon to treat allergy symptoms, such as runny nose and watery, itchy eyes.

Lemon was seized upon by the cosmetics industry because it contains alpha hydroxy acids (AHA), which reduce and prevent wrinkles. Dr. Hauschka used lemon to create rejuvenating and revitalizing baths that have a firming effect on the skin. Lemon supports the skin against the development of cellulite.

Rosemary *Rosemarinus officialis L*

Family: Lamiaceae/Labiatae

Rosemary originated in the Mediterranean region and is a lover of warm climates and sunshine. Ancient healers recognized rosemary for its love of the sun, which the plant captures in its tiny leaves and retains in its essential oils.

Whether used as a culinary herb, a medicinal plant, or an essential oil, rosemary rapidly improves circulation, warms the body, harmonizes the nervous system, and enhances digestion. As a medicinal herb, rosemary is traditionally used to treat abdominal pain, colic, gout, rheumatism, chronic weakness, and low blood pressure. It clears the stomach and digestive system of feelings of fullness, bloating, and cramping. It also relieves flatulence.

Rosemary is used in many types of skin care products. When used in shampoo, it stimulates circulation in the scalp and improves the condition and strength of the hair. Rosemary essential oil can be purchased as a bath and body oil as well as an aromatherapy oil.

Sage *Salvia officinalis L*

Family: Lamiaceae (labiate plant)

Sage is a bush or a shrub with blue-violet flowers and slender leaves covered with a greenish-gray down. The strong smell of sage is released by rubbing the velvety surface. The flower appears to form the lips of a mouth from which the stamen emerges like a tongue. Native Americans burned sage and used it as a smudge to purify the aura fields and the bodies of people before they entered sacred ceremonies.

Sage is an anti-inflammatory, especially on the gums, mouth, and throat. It calms mucous membranes, relieves cramping, enhances digestion, and regulates perspiration. Sage originated in the Mediterranean, but it can withstand cold winters, a reflection of the strength of its life force, which it communicates in skin care products that contain it.

Sage is used in many skin care preparations, including acne-healing formulas, deodorants, body powders, and footbaths, where it purifies and draws stagnant emotions.

Saint-John's-Wort
Hypericum perforatum L
Family: Hypericaceae

The most remarkable distinguishing feature of Saint-John's-wort is the tiny luminous sacs that appear in its flower; these contain the essential oils. Rub the golden yellow flowers between your fingers; the oils will be released and immediately transformed by the light and oxygen into a bright red color.

Saint-John's-wort blooms between May and September. The woody stems and five-petaled flowers enjoy direct sunlight. The plant is native to Europe and Siberia and today grows all over the world.

Saint-John's-wort is most recognized as an herb that can relieve mild to moderate depression. Its essential oils are rich in antioxidants. Taken internally or applied directly, it can heal and close large pores and openings in the skin. It relieves pain, promotes healing of the skin and other tissues, and calms the nervous system. Saint-John's-wort is used by herbalists and homeopaths to treat all kinds of skin disorders, including chapped, cracked, or irritated skin, acne, and mild burns.

Witch Hazel
Hamamelis virginiana
Family: Hamamelidaceae

Witch hazel is a shrub that grows to more than 24 feet in height. In autumn, when all other plants appear to be shutting down for winter, witch hazel produces fragrant yellow flowers with narrow petals, reminding people of the inevitable return of spring. Witch hazel produces a long fruit that matures by the following summer and fall, which means that it produces flowers and fruit at the same time. When the fruit is finally ready, it bursts open at the top, spreading its seeds over a radius of several yards.

Witch hazel is highly astringent. It is also an anti-inflammatory and has potent antioxidant powers. It has been used traditionally to treat diarrhea and inflammation of the gums and mouth; to promote the healing of wounds, hemorrhoids, and varicose veins; and as a topical salve for all types of skin disorders. Witch hazel is among the most commonly used medicinal plants in skin care.

Chapter 3

The Skin

No organ reveals your physical beauty more than your skin. You may pride yourself on the shine in your hair or the color of your eyes, but no other feature gives you a greater experience of your beauty. All of us, at one time or another, have felt blessed by the beauty that can suddenly arise from our skin. We have also cringed when our skin inexplicably breaks out in a rash or blemishes. The skin is the part of us on which we are most commonly judged; it is also the part we most commonly examine to judge ourselves.

The skin performs a multitude of tasks, most of which go unnoticed and unappreciated. It protects us from disease and the daily onslaught of particles large and small. It cools us when we are hot and warms us when we are cold. It heals wounds inflicted on it, often without any assistance from us. It absorbs sunlight to produce vitamin D, essential to the health of our bones and teeth, keeps itself moist, slows its own aging, and, every day, attempts to renew and restore its beauty.

While skin accomplishes all of this on its own, it still needs help. With every blemish, rash, and wrinkle, the skin is asking us to understand its nature and to support its efforts at self-renewal. Unfortunately, many of us respond to changes in our skin with practices that, in fact, assault and injure it further, consequently accelerating the aging process. On the other hand, many of us do nothing at all for our skin—but nonetheless expect it to remain clear, beautiful, and young.

In order to create the most effective program for our skin, we must begin by understanding what it does each day and how best to support its work.

The Perfect Shield

Skin has three layers. The outermost layer, the part you see, is called the *epidermis.* The middle layer is called the *dermis,* and below the dermis lies the skin's foundation, called the *subcutaneous layer.* These three layers work in concert to form a healthy and beautiful skin.

The Epidermis

The epidermis is itself composed of layers, the top of which is your shield. As beautiful and as supple as the skin can be, it is also a form of armor. Let's face it; it's a tough world out there and you need armor to protect you from drying winds, rain and snow, dust and stone, sleet and hail, among many other hazards. The skin can take all that and a lot more. In fact, in some of the places on our bodies, such as our hands and feet, the skin develops hard, tough calluses to protect itself against intense wear.

The hard surface of the skin, known as the *horny layer* or *stratum corneum,* is made of dead cells that are flat and flexible. They originate at the bottom of the dermis, a region known as the *basal layer.* Once they are born, these cells migrate upward to the surface. On their way, they are transformed into protein-producing cells known as *keratinocytes.* Whenever the skin is cut or abraded, the job of keratinocytes is to signal the dermis to produce more cells so that the cut can be knitted together and the wound closed as quickly as possible. When they reach the surface and encounter the air, the keratinocytes die, forming your defense shield. After a week or two, they slough off, making way for another round of cells that forms a new horny layer. The journey from the basal layer to the surface of the skin takes about 28 days; this rate slows to 35 and 42 days and longer as we head into our senior years.

Before they die, keratinocytes act with surrounding cells to produce chemicals that regulate your immune system. If you get scratched or cut, or develop a boil, for example, these cells trigger an immune response that attacks bacteria and viruses that swoop into the open wound. Your immune system also helps cleanse the tissue of dirt and chemicals that infiltrate the opening. One of the by-products of an immune reaction is inflammation—the red swelling and heat that surrounds a wound.

Your immune system distinguishes your cells and those of invaders, assessing the aliens for possible danger to your health. The more poisons enter your system, the more vigorously your immune system responds and the more your tissues are inflamed, resulting in rapid aging.

Among the poisons we must avoid are synthetic substances placed on the skin. Every synthetic chemical used in skin care and beauty products has side effects for some percentage of the population. The more synthetics you use, the more rapidly your skin ages. I mentioned parabens in the last chapter; other common substances of concern include PEGs (polyethylene glycols), which cause rashes, skin irritations, and inflammation in sensitive people; phthalates, derivatives of the petrochemical naphthalene (the substance used in mothballs), which has been linked to birth defects and serious hormonal imbalances; and benzophenon, commonly used in sunblock, which causes irritation, inflammation, and skin rashes.

In general, synthetic substances have three potential effects on the epidermal and dermal layers. First, they can stimulate an allergic reaction, causing swelling of the sensitive tissues, including the eyes and sinuses. Second, they can cause irritation, which can result in an inflammatory reaction. Third, they can increase the permeability of the skin—in essence, poke holes in the epidermis—thus allowing more disease-causing agents to penetrate. The bottom line is that synthetic ingredients can wreak havoc on your skin and overtax your immune system. This is why you want to use skin care products that contain only natural ingredients.

Think of your epidermis as a living shield. It protects you from assaults from without while it guards the treasures within, among the most important of which is water. Well-hydrated skin maintains its plump, unlined youthfulness. Your epidermis makes sure your skin retains the moisture trapped within it, especially in the dermis. When the dermis is full of moisture, your skin is soft, dense, and pillowy. If not for the epidermis, the moisture in your skin would come to the surface and evaporate, leaving your skin dry, wrinkled, and aged. By keeping the skin hydrated, the epidermis maintains your natural moisturizing factor (NFM). People who have good NFM have a healthy epidermis. In fact, the better your epidermis, the greater your NFM.

Skin varies in sensitivity. It can be as tough as a fireman and as soft as a rose petal. One of the substances that give skin this beautiful and seemingly contradictory quality is sebum, an oil-like compound that coats the epidermis. Sebum is made of fatty acids, fatty alcohols, waxes, lactic acid, and salts. These constituents combine to give sebum a pH of between 4.3 and 6—meaning that it is slightly acidic, hence the term *acid mantle* for the coating of the skin. This acid base on your skin is highly effective at neutralizing bacteria and other disease-causing agents. Sebum also helps seal moisture into the skin. It's hard on germs but soft to the touch.

The epidermis also contains the cells that provide pigment, or melanocytes. Only about 2 or 3 percent of the cells in the epidermis are melanocytes, which means this tiny minority of cells provides all the color in our skin. When the epidermis is treated with harsh chemicals and peels, the melanocytes can become deformed, resulting in irregularities in skin color.

Any program that supports the epidermis, therefore, supports the health, youthfulness, and beauty of the skin. On the other hand, substances that injure the epidermis, or strip it from the skin, are actually helping to destroy the skin, even though it may appear to give a short-term benefit. Alpha hydroxy acids, for example, strip the upper layers of the epidermis and expose the soft tissue below. That may appear to enhance the skin's appearance for a short while, but in fact it accelerates the aging of the skin in the long run. Thus, we see the great divide in skin care approaches today. We either work with the skin to assist it in doing what it does best, or we end up injuring the skin, or replacing its normal function, for short-term benefits.

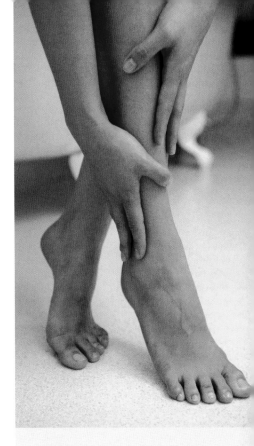

above The epidermis protects us from the elements.

below Healing plants work with the skin to help it achieve a state of balance.

The Dermis

The dermis might be thought of as a watery world. Living inside that world are blood and lymph vessels, small muscles, and nerves that convey our sense of touch. Also embedded in the dermis are sweat glands, hair follicles, and sebaceous glands, which produce sebum. The body is constantly resupplying the dermis with water to keep it moist, healthy, and beautiful.

Traversing the dermis are fibrous strands, about 80 percent of which are made of a protein called *collagen.* Collagen forms a dense matrix that protects the skin from splitting when it is pulled or twisted. The remainder of the strands are *elastin,* another protein-based fiber. Elastin acts like rubber bands; whenever the skin is pulled or stretched, elastin snaps it back into its original shape. As we age, however, the elastin weakens.

In youth, collagen and elastin are moist and plump, which makes the skin appear full, soft, and unlined. They give the skin its fullness and shape. As we age, the fibers are attacked by oxygen-free radicals, which causes them to dry, shrink, and cross-link with other collagen strands, forming structures that look like fishnetting. As the collagen base shrinks, the skin at the surface folds over on itself, forming wrinkles. Sometimes the collagen becomes so cross-linked that the skin itself looks like fishnetting. As discussed in chapter 2, the antidote to the problem of free radicals is the antioxidants found in plants. By eating antioxidant-rich plants and applying plant-based substances directly on your skin, you infuse the skin with antioxidants. These substances neutralize free radicals and slow the skin's aging process. Medicinal plants can heal the skin and restore much of its beauty and radiance.

The dermis is infused with blood vessels that bring oxygen and nutrition to nerves, glands, hair follicles, and cells, including those at the surface. When the body is cold, blood starts to move rapidly to bring in more warmth. When the body is hot, sweat glands start pumping moisture to the surface, where it evaporates and takes away some of the excess heat.

Also within the watery dermis lie waste products that are constantly being expelled from your cells and tissues. Those toxins are eliminated from your body by your lymph system. This is a complex network of vessels and nodes that absorbs intracellular waste particles from the gel-like fluid and takes it away to be neutralized by the liver and expelled by the kidneys. Within the lymph vessels and nodes are antibodies and immune cells, called *lymphocytes,* which destroy disease-causing agents.

Like any waste-removal system, the lymph works best when it is moving. When it is congested or blocked, waste builds up in the tissues and can cause blemishes, rashes, and irritations on the skin. Unlike the circulatory system, the lymph has no heart to help keep it moving. That job is left to you. You help keep your lymph circulating by moving your body, especially with exercise—walking, dancing, stretching, and yoga, for example. Needless to say, the better your lymph system is at removing toxic substances, the clearer and more beautiful your skin is.

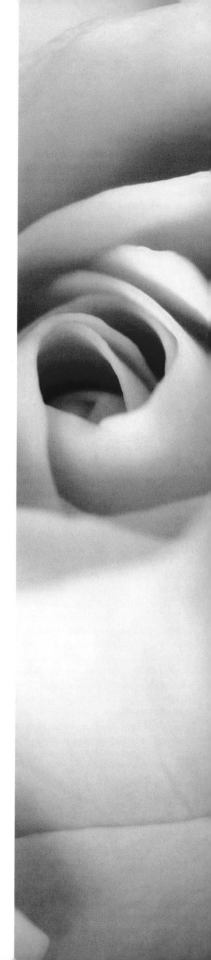

One way to reduce the burden on both your lymph and your skin is to reduce the toxic substances you ingest, especially through your diet. Try to avoid excess consumption of artificial substances, alcohol, animal fats, and cholesterol. Another way to keep your skin clear and the lymph unburdened is to stop smoking.

Deep within the dermis and down into the subcutaneous layer are hair follicles. The hairs that grow out of these follicles act like reeds in a pond. In the same neighborhood as the follicles are the sebaceous glands, which produce sebum. Along with the skin's water content, sebum moisturizes the skin. Once secreted, the sebum attaches itself to hairs and climbs upward to the surface along them to create the skin's soft yet protective acid mantle.

When the sebaceous glands are overactive, sebum can collect in the openings, or pores, of the skin, and in the places where the hairs appear at the surface. When this happens, pores and follicles can become blocked, infected, and inflamed, causing blemishes, boils, swelling, and scarring.

Also buried within the dermis are the sweat glands, which release moisture to cool the body. Sweat glands also eliminate waste, thus functioning as an adjunct to the kidneys and urinary tract.

The Subcutaneous Layer

Below the dermis is the subcutaneous layer, which contains fat, muscle, and some blood circulation. The fat and muscle act as a shock absorber for the skin, much as collagen does. At this layer, we find those annoying bands of cellulite, which is essentially fat, held in place by connective tissue lined with fat. Metabolic activities also take place here.

Ideally, diet and exercise habits promote both general health and the health and beauty of your skin. This thinking is the basis for a new approach to health care known as *salutogenesis,* or the act of promoting continual good health, as opposed to preventing or treating disease. A salutogenetic approach to skin care means using a health-promoting diet, lifestyle, and healing plants to help the skin perform its most basic and essential tasks.

Modern life has fostered a fragmented way of thinking that encourages us to see the parts of the body as separate from the organism as a whole. For example, there's no end to the number of beauty experts who will tell you how to have a beautiful face and clear skin but never mention the importance of the overall health of your body. Your commitment to being beautiful is really a commitment to your overall good health and vitality. Clear, radiant skin reflects good health. What most beauty experts won't tell you is that a beautiful face and radiant skin depend especially on the health of your kidneys and large and small intestines.

The Foundation of Healthy and Beautiful Skin

Rudolf Hauschka taught that the beauty of your skin, and the cause of all skin problems, could be revealed by understanding the threefold design of human beings.

Each of us has a nerve and sense function that gives us thinking and sensory abilities. Each of us is blessed with organs that work through rhythmic action, or coordinated expansion and contraction. These include the heart and lungs. Finally, we have digestive and metabolic functions—that is, the ability to absorb nutrients for cellular activity (metabolism) and the capacity to eliminate waste. The body is designed with the nervous system headquartered on the top floor, so to speak; the rhythmic system centered primarily in the chest (where the heart and lungs are); and the digestive system in the middle and lower thorax—the basement. Thus, these three systems permeate and integrate the activities of the body.

That same threefold nature can be seen in the skin as well. The upper layers are infused with nerve endings that tell us about the conditions in the environment. Our nerve and sense function has to be out in front if we are to have good intelligence about what's going on around us. Just below our nerve function are the capillaries, which bring blood, oxygen, and nutrients to the cells of the skin and correspond to the rhythmic organs, the heart and lungs. Below that are the lymph vessels and nodes, which remove waste from the skin. As the waste disposal function, the lymph system corresponds to our digestion. Hence, we find a general threefold nature in the overall body, and within the skin as well.

Dr. Hauschka said that whenever the skin is broken out in pimples or acne or a rash, the origin of the problem will be found not in the skin itself but in the waste disposal part of the body, or the digestive function. He saw that the skin attempts to discharge excess waste that cannot be eliminated through the normal channels, especially through digestion and the kidneys. Thus the skin is performing a function that should occur elsewhere in the body.

Therefore, in order to have beautiful skin, we must begin by caring for our kidneys and digestive function. The beauty of this understanding is that so much can be done in this area.

The form and function of certain healing plants mirror those of our skin.

Help Your Kidneys, Help Your Skin

The primary job of the kidneys is to remove the waste products of protein metabolism from the blood. These include nitrogen, uric acid (or urea), and ammonia. But the kidneys also remove many other toxins, including excess hormones, vitamins, minerals, food additives, drugs, and other foreign substances. In addition, they regulate the body's electrolyte balance, the array of minerals—including calcium, chloride, magnesium, phosphate, potassium, and sodium—needed for healthy nerve function. The kidneys are also involved in maintaining healthy blood pressure.

Finally, the kidneys regulate the amount of water in the body. When we consume too much liquid, the kidneys increase urination. When we drink too little, the kidneys retain water. Water, of course, keeps the moisture content of our skin at a high level.

Most of us don't consume enough pure, clean water. Tap water is often polluted with heavy metals and industrial chemicals. Not only are we water deprived, but many of us get all of our liquids in the form of coffee, tea, soda, fruit juice, and alcoholic beverages. All of these drinks can stress the kidneys, resulting in the loss of vital minerals and water. Coffee and soda, for example, are rich in phosphates and caffeine, which tax the kidneys and promote bone loss. Alcohol causes the body to be dehydrated and forces the kidneys to work hard to retain water. Meanwhile, many doctors and scientists have long known that excess consumption of animal proteins (more than 20 percent of calories per day) can damage the kidneys.

All of this means that if we are to have beautiful, well-hydrated skin, we must take good care of our kidneys by implementing the following practices:

1. Drink adequate amounts of pure spring water each day. Keep a large glass or a bottle of spring water at your desk and drink it throughout the day. Let your body tell you how much water you need by monitoring your reaction to the water you drink. As you drink, notice if your thirst becomes aroused and your body actually draws in the water. This is a sign that your body needs more water. Drink water morning, afternoon, and evening. This gives your body the opportunity to get all the water it needs, helping it eliminate waste products.

2. Get adequate sleep each night. You will notice that when you are exhausted, your skin is less radiant and more prone to blemishes and rashes. The kidneys are strengthened by rest and, more specifically, sleep. Six to eight hours of deep sleep per night allows the kidneys to adequately cleanse the blood, eliminating waste products that would otherwise be shunted to the skin. Try to establish a consistent rhythm between your waking and sleeping hours, especially if you lack vitality. Consider taking a short nap on the weekends, particularly when you are going through times of stress.

3. Consume appropriate—meaning low—amounts of sea salt (sodium chloride) and, for beautiful skin, avoid salty snacks. Health authorities recommend that we limit daily salt intake to about 500 milligrams (mg), or about 2 to 3 teaspoons. Try using celtic sea salt for its high mineral content.

Salt is only part sodium (the rest is chloride and other minerals). Food labels show sodium content, as opposed to salt content. Health experts recommend that we consume only 200 mg of sodium each day. A plant-based diet with regular consumption of animal foods provides all the sodium your body needs.

Salt consumption becomes excessive when we eat too many salty snacks and add salt to our foods. Excess salt consumption causes the kidneys to work overtime. Think back to the last time you had salty popcorn at the movies and had to urinate more than you're used to. Excess salt may result in bone loss, or osteoporosis. So if you have these conditions, I recommend that you avoid all salty snacks and refrain from adding salt or salty condiments, such as shoyu, tamari, or miso, at the table. Instead, cook with a pinch of sea salt and use low-sodium fermented foods. This, coupled with the naturally occurring sodium in your grains, vegetables, and animal foods, provides appropriate amounts of salt. Your kidneys will become stronger and your skin will glow.

above Control stress by finding your natural rhythms and engaging in healthy, supportive behaviors.

4. Control stress on the kidneys by finding your natural rhythms and engaging in the supportive behaviors described in chapter 1.

5. For the most beautiful skin, make plant foods your primary source of protein and supplement with small amounts of animal protein. The most abundant source of protein in the plant kingdom is beans and bean products, including tempeh and tofu, both soybean products. Some plant proteins are easier than animal foods for your kidneys to metabolize, while animal proteins increase urea, ammonia, and nitrogen, thus increasing the stress levels on your kidneys and skin. The diet provided in chapter 7 gives you all the plant and animal proteins your body needs while promoting beautiful skin.

6. Walk daily and, whenever possible, sweat. Exercise and sweat open the pores, promote deep breathing, and eliminate toxins that otherwise would be processed by the skin. Check out the sauna at your local health club or gym and try to take a sauna monthly or perhaps seasonally. Remember to cover the sensitive areas of your face with a thick cream when using a sauna or a steam bath.

7. Minimize your consumption of soft drinks and alcohol, and if you have any type of acute skin condition, eliminate soft drinks entirely. This is especially important for children and teenagers.

Heal Your Digestion and Your Skin Will Glow

As you support your kidneys, you should also strengthen your digestive function, which will further promote beautiful skin, by implementing the following practices:

1. Consume adequate water to promote healthy elimination and reduce the likelihood of constipation. One of the primary functions of the large intestine is to absorb water from digested food. When our water consumption is low, stools become dry, hard, and difficult to eliminate. The longer they reside inside the body, the more waste is drawn back into the bloodstream, whence it soon finds its way to the skin. This proves Dr. Hauschka's point—that constipation and other digestive imbalances force the skin to do the job of the digestive systems—and, in the process, reduce the beauty of our skin.

2. Eat cooked whole grains and vegetables daily for their high fiber content. High-fiber foods speed intestinal transit time, strengthen intestinal function, and can eliminate many disorders of the small and large intestines. If you are chronically constipated, add more water to your cooking to make your whole grains soft and moist. This will make them more digestible and easier to eliminate.

Many natural laxatives can promote healthy elimination. Senna tea is easily purchased. You can also prepare homemade remedies:

- Cook three or four figs, three or four prunes, and a small handful of raisins in apple juice at a low simmer until all the fruit is soft (less than 20 minutes). Eat the compote at night, three hours before bed.

- Upon rising, squeeze a quarter-wedge of fresh lemon into spring water and drink 30 minutes before eating or drinking anything else.

- Soak 2 tablespoons of flaxseed overnight. Eat the seeds upon waking the next morning. Chew thoroughly—roughly thirty-five times per mouthful.

3. Eat fermented foods to replace healthy flora. Most of us have taken antibiotics for one condition or another. These drugs kill disease but also destroy the friendly bacteria in your intestines that are the basis for healthy digestion. In addition, many kinds of environmental pollutants and dietary substances kill intestinal flora and weaken digestion as well. You can strengthen your intestinal function and restore the population of friendly bacteria by eating fermented foods. These include natural miso, a fermented soybean paste that is rich in friendly bacteria and used in Asian cooking to make soups, stews, and sauces (see the recipes in the back of this book for cooking with miso). Other sources of friendly bacteria include sauerkraut, pickles, and Japanese shoyu and tamari, both fermented liquid soybean products used in soups, stews, and sauces. Still

below Flaxseed aids in digestion.

left For the most beautiful skin, make plant foods your primary source of protein.

another wonderful fermented food is tempeh, an Asian soybean patty that can be fried or boiled as part of a noodle broth or soup.

4. Walk daily to work the abdominal muscles, massage the digestive tract, and promote healthy elimination. Try to walk at the same time every day to develop another healthy rhythm in your life. Walking regularly can help strengthen willpower and clear the mind. As an experiment, the next time you walk, ask yourself an important question regarding a problem you are facing. You may be able to see the answer clearly by the time you've finished your walk.

Take Care of the Basics First

These steps alone will have a dramatic effect on your skin, promoting its beauty and youthful vitality. They will also clear up many intractable skin disorders. But you can do much more to care for your skin. The next chapter shows how to care for your face and body daily so that your skin becomes beautiful and lustrous. Once you have a healthful daily skin care regimen in place, turn to chapter 5, where you'll find advanced treatments for healing specific skin problems.

Chapter 4

The Face

I believe that virtually all people can have an attractive and, on many days of the week, even a beautiful face. To be more specific, virtually everyone can have more beautiful facial skin, even those who have had problems with acne, rosacea, and even minor scarring. Everyone's face can radiate a certain soft illumination that we all intuitively recognize as an essential part of beauty. Everyone can present a face that reflects confidence, self-love, and inner harmony.

The question is, how? All of us who want to be more beautiful ask ourselves these questions: First, what creates facial beauty, and second, what practical steps can we take to enhance, amplify, and restore it?

Facial beauty is more complex than the beauty of, say, hands, hair, or feet. This is partly because your face expresses the music of your inner life. No other part of the body so directly reveals your thoughts, emotions, internal conflicts, and long-term psychological patterns. The emotions that dominate your inner self show up on your face. Anger or depression, for example, show on your face. Conversely, if you are emotionally balanced and essentially happy, that, too, shows up on your face. More subtle feelings are communicated on the face, as well. Conceit and rejection of others, or of oneself, give the face a certain cast. Seriousness, playfulness, self-confidence, compassion—all of these are etched on the face. They, too, can determine whether you are perceived as beautiful.

Your face also reveals how you take care of yourself—that is to say, your dietary and drinking habits, whether you smoke, exercise, get enough rest, and feel loved. Your face is the physical manifestation of your personality and spiritual condition. More than any other part of your body, your face reveals your true identity.

Over time, your inner life imprints itself on your face; the emotions, judgments, and beliefs that are sustained through the years become embedded in your features. Pessimism, anger, and frustration mold the face, as do optimism, hopefulness, and love. Take the same face, with all the same features. Mold it with anger and rage or reshape it with optimism and compassion. It's obvious which face is more beautiful.

Yes, we all attempt to cover up our inner feelings; we're entitled to our privacy, after all. The difference between a face that is true and authentic and one that is false or hostile is the degree to which the person is honest with herself about her feelings and her willingness to seek ways of healing her pain.

Inevitably, some days I will feel sad or angry; I will experience loss, or setbacks, or doubts about myself. The question is, how am I going to deal with these feelings? Am I going to look at why they have emerged or the events or memories that might have triggered them? Am I going to get help to heal my pain? Or am I going to wallow in my misery until it turns into more pain, deeper anger, and even depression?

Sadness, anger, and feelings of loss all cry out for help—or, more specifically, for caring and love. Each negative emotional state must be addressed and healed. We must be honest about what we feel and get help when it is really needed. That help may be as simple as a conversation with a partner or a friend. It could also be the essential work you do with a healer or a therapist. Whenever you decide to honestly confront your inner darkness, you are acting courageously, honestly, and with self-love. And that, as we all know, is beautiful—and will result in beauty.

People who have confronted their fears and pain and have applied the healing balm of love and tender care are rewarded with a special kind of beauty, one that appears on the face as the radiance of wisdom, love, and peace.

The Four Pillars of Beauty

All of which brings us to the first pillar of a beauty, which is truth. A beautiful face is an honest face. Not only does it reflect, to some degree, what is going on inside, but it also reveals a person who is honestly coping with whatever stresses she may be experiencing. A person who is in touch with her feelings and seeks the help and care she needs does not remain in a negative state for long. She has compassion for herself; she seeks help and healing; and she wants the same for others.

Which brings us to the second pillar of beauty—goodness. One of the first traits we all seek in another person's face is the capacity to love. We know to stay away from someone whose face is full of anger, rage, or hate. But a face that radiates love, and is lovable, reveals a person who is essentially good. Truth, goodness, and love combine to create beauty.

Truth, goodness, and love (the third pillar of beauty) are the guiding principles we must apply as we care for our faces. There is little honesty or goodness in synthetic ingredients, many of which injure our skin and speed up the aging process. The effects of these products can hardly be considered an act of love. Nor is beauty bestowed on the faces of those who neglect their skin. Beauty arises when we treat our skin with substances that support its health and with gentle, loving care.

To truth, goodness, and love, we can add the fourth pillar of beauty, nature, which embodies these three great forces of life. Nature's healing foods and medicinal plants are the physical manifestation of truth, goodness, and love. Skin care products that are made from nature's healing plants bring forth and magnify our beauty. Indeed, they are the sources of true beauty.

Holistic Versus Conventional Skin Care

Many, if not most, conventional skin care products are developed in response to the belief that your skin is misbehaving and therefore must be managed or even coerced into acting properly. In essence, the skin is a recalcitrant child and often even the enemy. Drugs and other forms of medicine are needed to force the body to function properly and the skin to look healthy. However, as you know, the more extreme the medicine, the greater the side effects. Very often, harsh skin care products cause us to exchange one set of problems for another.

Holistic skin care sees the body as an integrated unit in which every function works together to achieve the harmony that is health. One of the consequences of health is beautiful skin. Rather than seeing the body as the enemy, the holistic approach views the body as a wise friend who must be understood and supported. We must learn from the body and act in harmony with its basic behaviors and laws.

A healing diet, competent digestion, regular exercise, and a commitment to achieving emotional harmony all combine to create glowing skin and a beautiful face. On the other hand, the more out of balance our lives are in any of these areas, the more our skin suffers and the more we depend on conventional products and potions.

A good illustration of the very different types of thinking that underlie the conventional versus the holistic approaches to skin care is AHAs, or alpha hydroxy acids.

Alpha hydroxy acids (AHAs) were originally derived from the acids in plants and milk products. Today, virtually all of the AHAs on the market are synthetically produced and are far more powerful than their natural predecessors. AHAs have different effects on the skin depending on the concentration. At concentrations of 3 percent or lower, AHAs bind with water and hold it to the surface of the skin, thus acting as a moisturizer. At concentrations of 4 percent or more, AHAs break down the adhesive substance that holds cells in place within the stratum corneum and cause these dead cells to slough off, exposing the living cells below. The living cells look younger and brighter, which is part of the reason AHAs have become so popular. Unfortunately, synthetic AHAs often injure the stratum corneum and the acid mantle, leaving the skin unprotected and vulnerable to environmental assault. Moreover, without a strong stratum corneum, the skin loses moisture and ages more quickly. This usually results in a dependence on moisturizers and other products—but these products can never compensate for the moisture loss and consequent aging that occur when the skin is injured. Strong AHAs can also irritate mucous membranes.

AHAs have, however, been shown to be effective in the treatment of light-damaged skin, and some reports claim they can help people suffering from thickening of the skin caused by hyperkeratinization (excess production of keratinocytes). AHAs do have their place, but only when they are used in a balanced way and as part of a holistic approach to skin care.

Concentration is the all-important factor. Natural products, derived from medicinal plants, fruits, and milk products, possess AHAs in safe and appropriate concentrations at which the AHAs serve as good moisturizers or mild exfoliants. The cells that are exfoliated are most likely those that were ready to slough off from the stratum corneum. The stratum corneum and the acid mantle are left intact. Synthetic AHAs tend to be more concentrated and therefore more injurious to the skin.

This is just one of the many reasons to avoid synthetic products. They often have severe side effects and tend to do more harm than good. This rule should be followed strictly with respect to facial products. Plant-based skin care products contain an abundance of antioxidants and other plant compounds that reduce oxidation and inflammation, the two processes that age the skin. As I discussed in chapter 2, many plant substances heal the skin. Plus, plants contain that indefinable etheric or life energy, or what the Chinese call *chi*. Chi arises from overall health and from healthy skin. It is also enhanced by the chi in living substances that you apply to your face.

The second rule is to touch your face with gentle, loving care. Don't scrub your face or treat it harshly. Your face is the physical manifestation of your inner life. When you treat your face with healing love, gentleness, and compassion, you are treating your inner life in the same way. You are actually healing your own heart when you care for your face with love. And in a very short time it shows. Soon, the care and love you give your face spreads to other aspects of your life.

Here is a short exercise to illustrate my point. Close your eyes and gently place your hands on your face. Take a deep breath, exhale, and release as much tension from your face and body as you can. Feel the intimacy you suddenly have with yourself. Now, very gently, with the tips of your fingers, massage your forehead. Do this with great care, running your fingertips across your eyebrows and then down along the orbital bones around your eyes. Move to your cheekbones, massaging gently and lovingly. Feel your facial muscles start to relax and let go of tension. Move your fingertips along the bridge of your nose, to the nose itself, and then to your upper lip. With a very light touch, massage your lips and the muscles around your mouth. Feel every facet of your face. As you massage your face, notice how other areas of your body, especially your lower back and pelvis, let go of tension. Move your fingertips to your cheeks and very lightly massage them in a clockwise fashion. Move your hands to the back of your jawbone, right beneath your ears, and gently massage the jawline from the back to the chin. As you massage your face, notice that your hands and fingertips are filling with life energy that is then conferred to your face. Continue to breathe. Move your hands down to below your chin and massage below your neckline, gently pulling the flesh of your lower chin toward your neck. Massage the sides and back of your neck, paying particular attention to the area at the back of your head, where your skull and spine join. Place your hands back over your face and take a moment in the silence. Relax. Take your hands away from your face and open your eyes. Notice how you feel. Aren't you more connected with yourself? Don't you feel a little more relaxed, a little more soothed, and a little more comforted? Your face can be a gateway to your heart. Treat your face with loving-kindness, and you will encourage the healing of your heart.

The Beauty Basics

To heal the beauty of your face, begin with four basic steps: cleansing, toning, moisturizing, and appropriate night care. General guidelines for each of these four steps follow; these show how adhering to this regimen can restore the beauty of your face and start to heal the common disorders associated with it. You can use any cleansing, toning, or moisturizing product you currently enjoy or feel is working for you. For those who want to experiment with new healing substances, two sets of formulas are included for each step. The first set is an array of generic healing compounds that you can make yourself, to cleanse, tone, and moisturize your face. These formulas are extremely effective, low-cost herbal remedies for healing your skin. The medicinal plants recommended have been used for centuries—in some cases, millennia.

The second set of recommendations cover Dr. Hauschka Skin Care Products, which are all natural and contain no artificial ingredients. They incorporate the most powerful and effective medicinal plants available. The plants are raised biodynamically and subjected to a rhythmical extraction method that preserves their life energy.

These four basic steps, and the healing remedies provided, can help restore beauty and heal specific skin conditions, such as oily or dry skin, acne, and rosacea.

Step 1. Cleansing Your Face

Cleansing your face is the most important step in your skin care regimen. During the night, as you sleep, the body is actively engaged in healing itself. You know this firsthand, since many times you go to bed with a fresh cut or sore and wake up the next morning to find the injury largely healed. As the body heals itself, it gathers waste products and sources of disease and tries to eliminate them through the urinary tract, the breath, the mouth, and the skin. Even though you brush your teeth before bed, you still must do it again in the morning because of all that has been eliminated through your mouth during the night. This is a sign that your body is working to restore your health.

The same process is taking place on the surface of your skin. When you wake in the morning, layers of toxins are sitting on the surface. Morning cleansing removes them and allows your skin to breathe freely again. Cleansing also promotes blood circulation, cell renewal, and the free flow of sebum to the surface. Among the jobs that sebum performs, of course, is to sustain the acid mantle, part of our defense against disease.

The skin is a self-regulating system that is continually attempting to produce just the right amount of sebum, or oil, and thus keep itself properly moisturized.

Keeping the skin clean allows it to regulate and balance its oil production.

With the pores open and unblocked, keratinocytes can migrate freely to the surface and replace the stratum corneum, the hard surface that guards against antagonists in the environment while keeping moisture locked into our tissues.

All of these natural efforts, supported by cleansing, combine to keep the skin healthy, vital, and free of any blemishes and acne.

How to Cleanse the Skin

1. Start by cleansing your face in either a warm shower or a basin of warm water. Warm water relaxes the skin and softens and opens the pores, thus allowing a deep cleaning to occur. The warmth also stimulates circulation, which in turn quickens the lymph—thus removing more waste from the tissues—and increases the flow of oxygen and nutrients to cells. This enhances the health of the skin and supports its efforts at eliminating waste both within its tissues and at the surface.

2. Use your hands in a press-and-roll motion to cleanse properly. Press the warm water and cleanser into your skin and then undulate, or roll, your hands so that as you draw your fingers and palms away from your face, you create a gentle suction that pulls or lifts dirt, oils, and dead cells away from your pores and skin surface. Imagine the skin releasing its impurities and tension into the water, which washes them away.

All motions are done lovingly and compassionately. When you touch your face, you are touching the most tender part of your identity. Treat it with kindness and understanding. Do not rub or scrub the skin, either with your hands or a cloth. It's an old wives' tale that scrubbing makes the skin bright and healthy. In fact, particles of dirt and pollution have sharp edges that, when rubbed into the skin, actually injure cells and create inflammation. Also, you don't want to rub the skin squeaky clean. Such scrubbing razes parts of the stratum corneum and removes much of the acid mantle, leaving the skin less protected than it was before you cleaned it.

The press-and-roll technique doesn't rub in dirt or pollutants but rather protects cells that are still healthy and doing their job. Thus, any exfoliation that occurs is natural, not a forced event.

Whenever the skin undergoes excess exfoliation, it is forced to speed up metabolic activities, partly because it must produce new cells to replace its protective shield, the stratum corneum. It must also produce more sebum to replace the acid mantle. All of this combines to make the skin's normal life cycle race, at least for a time. Soon, the skin is suffering from increased sensitivity—excess exfoliation is rough treatment on living tissue—and the sebum either becomes excessive or dries up altogether. Excessive sebum usually results in blemishes and acne. Slow production of sebum results in dry, brittle, thin skin. Either way, you've accelerated the aging process and left your skin in worse shape than it was before the exfoliation.

I am not against gentle exfoliation; but be mindful, as most exfoliants today are composed of harsh, synthetic chemicals that do more harm than good.

3. The next step in cleansing your skin is to rinse properly. Cup your hands with warm water and rinse thoroughly. The dirt, dead cells, and oils that the skin is ready to release are all bound up in the cleanser. Thus, rinsing away the cleanser removes the impurities from the skin.

   As you know, if a cleanser is not properly removed, the skin tightens and feels uncomfortable. When properly cleansed and rinsed, the skin is relaxed, moist, and sufficiently oiled, which makes it comfortable to live in and capable of doing its many jobs.

4. Finish with a cool compress. Have you ever noticed how much your face and head like cool water? Your hands may tell you that the water is too cool for comfort, but when the same water is applied to your face, the temperature often feels just right. The reason? Heat rises to the face and head to escape from the body. This is one of the reasons why it's a good idea to wear a hat in winter—to trap heat and thus keep your body warm. But the heat in the face is often caused by inflammation, which accelerates aging. The cool water dampens the fires of inflammation and promotes healing.

Herbal Skin Cleansers

Look for a skin cleanser that is composed of plant substances and is free of surfactants—substances that emulsify oils and gather dirt particles, which are rinsed away with water. Common soaps are surfactants. The problem with them is that they are highly alkaline and strip away the acid mantle of your skin, leaving it dry and unprotected. Many face and body washes made of plant compounds are available. Watch out for cleansers that contain synthetic fragrances and other substances that are irritating and often allergenic. Buy products that are natural and "synthetic fragrance free." If you prefer scented products, look for those that use essential oils. Another group of substances to avoid are synthetic preservatives, such as parabens, PEGs, and propylene glycol, which can cause skin reactions in many people, especially those with sensitive skin.

Here is an excellent generic skin cleanser that you can make yourself. It can be used on most types of skin to protect, softly exfoliate to remove only dead cells, and moisturize.

Alternatively, Dr. Hauschka Cleansing Cream can be used daily. Composed of sweet almond meal and extracts of anthyllis, calendula, chamomile, Saint-John's-wort, and witch hazel, the cleansing cream acts as a gentle exfoliant.

Almond Cleanser

Purchase coarsely ground organic or biodynamically produced almond butter. Mix 1 teaspoon almond butter with a little spring water to make a paste and apply it to your face as you would ordinary soap. The almond cleanser will wash away dirt and other impurities and preserve the skin's acid mantle. The oil in the almond butter will not clog pores. This cleanser is sufficiently gentle for people with dry or sensitive skin, but it is also healing, mildly exfoliating, and revitalizing for skin with blemishes and acne.

To make the product even more effective, soothing, and hydrating, add oat flour or oat bran that has been coarsely ground in a coffee grinder or a blender. Simply grind the oats and add them to the almond butter and spring water mix. The oats will soothe, moisturize, and act as a gentle exfoliant. Oats, like almond butter, contain vitamin E and other antioxidants that promote healing as they cleanse.

Yet another healing substance that can be added to the almond butter and spring water mix is medicinal clay powder (do not use potter's clay). You can purchase healing clay in any natural foods or health foods store. Clay absorbs impurities and detoxifies. Adding 1 tablespoon clay to the basic mix yields a powerful and extremely healing combination that will cleanse, moisturize, and purify your skin. If necessary, add more water to produce a rich, soothing mixture.

When cleansing the skin, gently press and roll. Avoid the eye area. Rinse well.

Cleansing Your Face

Dr. Hauschka Cleansing Cream is a daily cleansing formula composed of sweet almond meal and extracts of anthyllis, calendula, chamomile, Saint-John's-wort, and witch hazel, along with other healing plants. The almond meal acts as a gentle exfoliant, removing dirt, impurities, and dead skin and leaving the face feeling fresh and alive. Meanwhile, the medicinal plants moisturize, protect, and heal. They also stimulate the skin's own healing functions so the skin is actively engaged in promoting its own health long after you have washed your body and face. The cream can be used for all types of skin conditions on the face, neck, and décolleté.

Put ½ inch or more of Cleansing Cream in the palm of your hand; mix with warm water and apply to the face, earlobes, and décolleté. When using Cleansing Cream on the face, do not rub or scrub. Rather, moisten the face with warm water first and then press and roll the Cleansing Cream gently onto it, as if giving yourself a soft massage. Rinse with warm water and then with cool water.

Step 2. Toning and Strengthening Facial Skin

Toner completes the cleansing process. At a minimum, toner helps rinse away any residual cleanser from your skin. At the same time, it should strengthen your skin, promote elasticity, and tighten pores. Some toners can also cause your moisturizer to penetrate more deeply and enrich the dermal layers of your skin. Toners that contain medicinal herbs can help treat various types of skin conditions, including acne and rosacea. Adults and teenagers with blemishes or acne can benefit tremendously from a healing toner because it removes excess oils and dead cells that can clog pores. Dr. Hauschka Facial Toner can help heal all types of skin conditions, including both oily and dry skin as well as acne and rosacea.

Be careful of commercial toners. Many contain synthetic solvents; salicylic acid, a compound found in aspirin; and propylene glycol, a petroleum by-product that's also used in antifreeze and brake fluid. Needless to say, petrochemicals irritate and cause allergic reactions in many people.

When applying toner, use the press-and-roll hand motion. Do it with the same loving gentleness with which you applied your cleanser. Imagine your skin brightening and tightening as it becomes healthier and more alive.

Homemade Herbal Toners

You can make effective toners that will help heal any type of skin condition. The basic, general formula is simply to add medicinal herbs to organic or biodynamically produced apple cider vinegar and water. Place dried herbs loosely at the bottom of a mason jar; fresh herbs can loosely fill the jar. Pour warm apple cider vinegar over any of the herbs listed on the next page. Allow the mixture to sit for 2 weeks. Strain off the herbs and bottle the vinegar.

Add 2 tablespoons herbal vinegar to 1 pint water. (For sensitive skin, add only 1 tablespoon to 1 pint water.) Stir and apply to your face after cleansing. Choose any of the following herbs to combine with the vinegar.

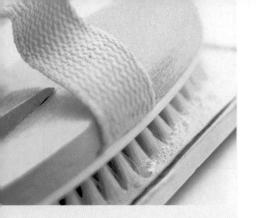

Body Wash

When it comes to getting clean, it's not about the bubbles. Bigger bubbles and foamy suds may be fun, but they don't necessarily wash away dirt. In fact, bubbles may indicate that your sudsy cleanser is loaded with harsh, synthetic cleansing agents. People have always sought better ways to cleanse. The first cleansers were natural materials like clay, sand, or nut meals that absorbed oil and dirt. Plants with surfactant or soaplike properties were also used.

Surfactants are natural or synthetic cleansers that allow water and oil to mix, thus emulsifying and removing dirt. Since the first bar of soap was made, surfactants have been designed and redesigned in our efforts to be squeaky clean.

Today, many surfactants are effective cleansers, but they irritate the skin. They are made with harsh manufacturing methods and toxic, nonrenewable materials. Gentle surfactants from natural, nontoxic sources are the best choice of ingredients for cleansing the body. Surfactants manufactured using simple procedures with plant-derived, biodegradable materials result in a light, creamy lather that washes away dirt and oils without irritating even the most sensitive skin.

Herb-Infused Vinegar Toners

Aloe vera (juice or gel). Traditionally used to treat all types of skin problems, especially cuts, abrasions, wounds, and burns, aloe speeds healing and prevents scarring. The gel is drawn from the pulpy aloe leaves. This herb, which was used by the ancient Egyptians and ever since, is safe, highly effective, and increasingly found in products from skin lotions to shampoos.

Aloe juice and vinegar make a very soothing and healing wash for sunburned and sensitive skin. Just slice open aloe leaves and scrape the juice into a bottle containing water and 1 to 2 tablespoons vinegar. Put in a spray bottle and keep in the refrigerator for up to two weeks. Use as a cooling mist.

Burdock. Burdock root is used by Native American and European healers to support and enhance the health of the kidneys, lungs, liver, and skin. It is highly effective at treating common skin problems. Burdock is frequently combined with dandelion and echinacea to boost the immune system, heal skin problems, and treat infections and fungus.

Chamomile. Chamomile is soothing to the face, especially sensitive skin.

Echinacea. Echinacea is a natural antibiotic, antibacterial, anti-inflammatory herbal plant used for centuries, especially in Europe. It boosts the immune system, promotes digestion, and heals infections. Echinacea is sold as a dried herb and as a tincture. It has no known contraindications. Echinacea can be combined with other herbs to treat skin irritations and infections, including blemishes. Highly recommended for treating acne.

Goldenseal. Goldenseal is an ancient medicinal plant that is an anti-inflammatory and an astringent. Goldenseal reduces inflammation, dries mucous membranes, regulates the menstrual cycle, cleanses the blood, promotes liver function, aids digestion, and treats bacterial infections. Highly recommended for treating rosacea and acne.

Yarrow. Yarrow has astringent properties and is used traditionally to treat skin disorders including pimples, acne, infections, itching, rashes, and other irritations. It is healing and an anti-inflammatory. Highly recommended for treating rosacea and acne.

The combination of echinacea, goldenseal, yarrow, and chamomile is highly recommended as a medicinal toner for treating acne, rosacea, and other sensitive or oily skin conditions. These herbs can heal your skin of many conditions. They are gentle, immune-boosting, and highly effective.

Lavender. Lavender essential oil, with its soothing qualities, promotes healing. Especially recommended for sensitive skin conditions.

Rosemary. Rosemary, combined with apple cider vinegar and some of the above mentioned herbs, makes a wonderful rinse for the hair and scalp. It can promote circulation and healing of the scalp.

These infused vinegars will keep unrefrigerated for up to six months.

For Your Body

Dr. Hauschka Body Wash Fresh contains a variety of moisturizing plant oils, and extracts of blackthorn, witch hazel, and essential oils from lemon and grapefruit. It removes dirt and excess oils, while moisturizing and revitalizing the skin.

Dr. Hauschka Body Wash Fresh elicits your skin's own moisturizing function. In fact, it does it so effectively that you may soon find that you no longer need to use a daily moisturizer on your body. It can be used for all types of skin conditions, including dry, irritated, or blemished, on the entire body.

Alternatively, Dr. Hauschka Facial Toner contains essential oils, anthyllis, and witch hazel, extracted as essences in water and alcohol, in a formula designed to improve the acid mantle and strengthen the skin's structure and elasticity. It is part of the Dr. Hauschka approach to healing rosacea and other skin conditions. It is also used for dry, sensitive, and normal skin types.

Step 3. Moisturizing Your Skin to Keep It Healthy and Full

When used properly, moisturizer adds to the moisture content of the skin to keep it soft, flexible, and full.

Moisturizers work primarily by creating a barrier on the skin that keeps moisture from evaporating from the surface. Each day we lose pints of water through evaporation from the skin. The drier the air, the more moisture is lost and the more the skin dries out. Needless to say, this accelerates aging. In effect, a good moisturizer does what the stratum corneum is meant to do: keep moisture inside the skin.

above Delicate, resilient, and balanced, the rose offers us a model for perfect skin.

Unfortunately, moisturizing is among the most misunderstood aspects of skin care. Many people believe that the more moisturizer they put on their skin, the more moisture will get into their skin. Actually, only minute amounts of moisture from the moisturizer itself get inside the skin.

Also, people either don't know or forget that the best any product can do is to help the skin do the job it is already doing. The skin has a built-in moisturizing system that is constantly attempting to regulate its own moisture content. We don't want to replace the skin's function. Rather, we want to support it and even strengthen it where we can.

Here's a basic rule of the body that we should keep in mind when using moisturizers: Use it or lose it—meaning if we do not use the body's inherent functions and abilities, we will lose them. If we overwhelm the skin's efforts to moisturize by applying excess moisturizer, we weaken the skin's ability to moisturize itself. That will make it dependent on external moisturizers. Even worse, sooner or later the skin will dry up anyway, despite all the moisturizer slathered on it, because it will have lost its ability to sustain optimal moisture within its own tissues. The use-it-or-lose-it rule is pretty much universal. If you don't exercise your bones, for example, they weaken and become porous. If you don't exercise your muscles, they atrophy. If you use laxatives instead of eating fibrous foods, your intestines become dependent on laxatives to work at all. In the same way, if you use too much moisturizer, the skin's natural moisturizing function becomes overwhelmed and weakens. Moisturizers that contain medicinal plants, especially those I have described, not only moisturize but also heal the skin and promote its own moisturizing abilities.

We often burden the skin even further when we believe, incorrectly, that the skin does the same work during the day that it does at night. During the day, the skin naturally produces more oil in order to protect itself against environmental insults—big swings in temperature, the overwhelmingly dry air in which most of us work, and bombardment by pollutants and particles of dirt. At the same time, the skin's antioxidant defenses are directed against the impact of the sun's ultraviolet rays and other sources of oxidation, such as chemical pollutants. Meanwhile, bacteria and viruses attack the skin but are neutralized by the acid mantle.

All of this points to the fact that during the day, the skin needs protection from external forces. A good moisturizer provides much of that protection, not only keeping the moisture within the skin but also strengthening the acid mantle.

At night, while you sleep, the skin shifts gears and performs an entirely new set of tasks: It heals itself. With the body at rest, the skin utilizes the nutrients consumed during the day—especially the plant-based antioxidants and phytochemicals—to restore, renew, and replace cells and tissues. It works hard and, not surprisingly, breathes hard. The skin breathes through the pores. At the same time, it's getting rid of waste products that were gathered during the healing process and are now expelled through the pores and hair follicles. This is all part of the skin's job. You don't want a lot of moisturizer or oils clogging your pores while you sleep because it will only increase the likelihood of blocked passageways, blackheads, pimples, and other skin eruptions. Skin should be free to breathe and eliminate optimally and efficiently. In sum, we want to have different approaches to daytime and nighttime skin care and moisturizing.

Daytime Moisturizing

Daytime is when moisturizer is important. Most moisturizers contain some form of oil. There are four general types. The first group is plant-based moisturizers, derived from a remarkably diverse array of plants including almonds, avocados, coconut, jojoba, olives, palm, sesame and sunflower seeds, and wheat germ. Plant oils penetrate the skin's surface and add moisture to the skin.

The second type is moisturizers made with animal fats—primarily fish oils, cholesterol, and lanolin. I don't recommend animal fats because they do not break down easily and often clog the pores, resulting in blemishes, acne, and other skin disorders. Also, animals consume and are treated with a wide array of highly toxic substances. Those poisons collect in the animal fat and can be transferred to the skin through products made from animals raised by conventional livestock methods.

below Moisturizers work primarily by creating a barrier to protect and support the skin.

left At night, while you sleep, the skin shifts gears to restore, renew, and replace cells.

The third type, mineral oil–based moisturizers, is derived from petroleum. These moisturizers are heavy and tend to clog the pores and block elimination. Further, they are difficult to remove from the skin without heavy soap. They also trap heat from the sun and atmosphere and raise the temperature of the skin, resulting in inflammation. People with sensitive skin often react negatively to mineral oils and suffer blemishes and acne.

The last group is vitamin E–oil moisturizers, also known as *tocopherols.* Vitamin E is an antioxidant that neutralizes free radicals, protects skin cells, and slows the aging process. Vitamin E tocopherol oils are derived from a variety of plants, most often alfalfa, almond oil, fennel, and wheat germ. They can also be produced synthetically, but you should avoid the synthetic version, because it very likely will not have the same degree of potency nor protective effects. If you use vitamin E oil, make sure it's from plant sources, such as wheat germ oil, as opposed to a synthetic version.

Some common moisturizers do not use any oils. These are called *humectants.* They can draw moisture to your skin from the environment, but the effect can also backfire and draw moisture from the dermal layer of your skin. People with acne tend to react better to humectants than to oils.

Always choose organic or biodynamic plant-based products. In addition, use any of the moisturizing masks described below, each of which can be applied in the evening and rinsed away before bed. These masks contain antioxidants and phytochemicals that not only hydrate but also purify the skin. They are also easy to make.

Alternatively, the Dr. Hauschka approach to daytime moisturizing is to help the skin hold in moisture, support the skin's own moisture-producing activities, and heal the skin of blemishes or other disorders. Dr. Hauschka daytime moisturizers include:

Avocado Mask

This is a wonderful moisture replenisher for the skin.

Mash half an avocado (preferably biodynamically or organically grown).

Apply a layer about $1/8$ inch thick to your clean face and let sit for 20 to 30 minutes. Rinse well with warm water and a facecloth.

Strawberry Yogurt Mask

This mask hydrates and brightens the face. The strawberries and yogurt contain small amounts of natural fruit and lactic acids, which hydrate and gently exfoliate the skin. These AHAs are less concentrated than commercial alpha hydroxy acids, which are often synthetic and very powerful, and therefore do not damage the epidermis. The mild acids also help soften the appearance of pigmentation problems. They can fade freckles and age spots as well.

Evenly spread $1/4$ cup strawberry yogurt (organic or biodynamic, if possible) over a clean face, avoiding the eye area. Let sit for 20 to 30 minutes. Tissue off and rinse well.

Honey Mask

This mask hydrates and purifies. Honey is used traditionally to heal and moisturize the skin.

Spread raw honey over a clean face, avoiding the eye area. Let sit for 20 to 30 minutes. In order to promote pore cleansing, tap your figures lightly around the areas of the skin where pores may be clogged. This action creates tiny suctions that help dislodge clogged pores and blackheads. Rinse well with warm water.

Dr. Hauschka Moisturizing Day Cream

For normal, dry, or mature skin. Moisturizing Day Cream is a light, activating moisturizer for men and women that balances the water and oil content of the skin. It contains nurturing essential oils along with healing medicinal plants, including anthyllis, witch hazel, carrot, Saint-John's-wort, and calendula. This formula is designed to restore color, freshness, and vitality to pale, dry skin and to reinvigorate the skin's own healing and moisturizing functions. Apply a small amount of Moisturizing Day Cream in the mornings to the face and neck. This cream activates the sebaceous glands to produce oil.

Dr. Hauschka Rose Day Cream

For dry or sensitive skin. A rich moisturizer that renews and protects the delicate outer layer of skin, it contains extracts of rose petal, rose hip, and avocado.

Dr. Hauschka Quince Day Cream

For normal, dry, or sensitive skin. A light, refreshing cream for men and women that helps maintain a balanced, healthy skin. Quince Day Cream contains quince seed extract, quince wax, and beeswax. These substances combine to hydrate and protect the skin. Apply over Moisturizing Day Cream to provide extra protection for a dry skin condition.

Dr. Hauschka Normalizing Day Oil

For oily or blemished skin. This moisturizer contains a wide array of therapeutic botanicals, plant extracts, and oils. The formula, which is rich in antioxidants and medicinal plant substances, regulates the overproduction of oil, reduces blemishes and pore size, and heals the skin of blemishes and acne. Oily skin becomes normalized.

Dr. Hauschka Toned Day Cream

For normal, dry, or sensitive skin. A rich, tinted moisturizer that blends skin tone, offering a transparent healthy glow. Calms red, irritated skin and conditions of couperose and rosacea. Apply over Moisturizing Day Cream to provide extra protection for a dry skin condition.

Step 4. Night Care

You should not put moisturizers or oils on your face at night. I realize that this is contrary to what many people believe, but the truth is that putting moisturizers or oil on your face at night is contrary to what your body is trying to do while you sleep. Ideally, night care for the face should support the skin's efforts to heal and eliminate waste products. The simplest way to accomplish this is to wash the face thoroughly in the evening with one of the herbal cleansers described earlier. Follow that with one of the hydrating and purifying masks on page 82. After wearing the mask for twenty to thirty minutes, wipe it off, cleanse, and rinse. Go to bed wearing nothing else on your face. When you wake up in the morning, use one of the cleansers to eliminate the toxins expelled during the night.

Alternatively, Dr. Hauschka Rhythmic Night Conditioner is a product especially designed to assist the skin's efforts to heal and eliminate at night. Rhythmic Night Conditioner balances all skin conditions, encourages cell renewal, improves strength and elasticity, restores moisture balance, and brings color and vitality to pale, lifeless skin. Among its ingredients is royal jelly, the rarefied form of honey made by worker bees and fed to the queen bee, which encourages transformation and regeneration of the skin. The product also contains essential oil of rose, which helps the skin renew and regenerate the epidermis; witch hazel, which cleanses, activates pores, tightens the skin, tones and strengthens tissues; and other healing substances. If you choose to use this product, I recommend you do it over a twenty-eight-day period. If you use it consistently, you will see remarkable changes in your skin and a reemergence of your beauty.

A Holistic View of the Face

For most of us, the places where blemishes and wrinkles appear on the face seem altogether random and chaotic. Why do I break out on my forehead? some of us ask, while others wonder why they break out around their mouth, or nose, or on their cheeks. Most doctors and conventional health experts cannot answer these questions, but for a traditional healer—one schooled in the ancient arts of diagnosis—the face is a precise map of the entire body. Individual features—the forehead or the nose, for example, or the area below the eyes or around the mouth—indicate the health and function of specific organ systems.

Dr. Hauschka applied his threefold lens to the face and showed that each of the three regions of the face correspond to the three primary functions of the body.

The Forehead

The forehead represents the sense and nervous system functions, including thinking. If someone has an abundance of lines (more than five) on the forehead, with many of them shallow and broken, this may indicate that he or she is using far too much energy thinking, as opposed to acting instinctively or from the heart. Broken lines can indicate thoughts that are not well organized or complete but rather stray in several directions without coming to a conclusion.

Blemishes and pimples on the forehead indicate excessive thinking that may be drawing life energy away from the digestive system, thus weakening elimination function and increasing the level of toxins in the bloodstream. In this case, the answer is to stop obsessing or thinking too much. Enjoy life. Participate in physical activities and allow instinctive and emotional centers to regain their balance.

In order to reduce thinking and strengthen the intestines, do the following:

- Eat more cooked whole grains, such as brown rice, millet, barley, and oats.
- Make sure to consume enough water.
- Increase consumption of leafy, green, and root vegetables to strengthen intestinal function.
- Walk daily.
- Avoid processed foods, especially those with little or no fiber.
- Treat constipation with natural means.
- Decrease caffeine consumption.
- Engage in some type of artistic expression.

Drink As Much Water As Your Body Needs

You use a moisturizer to keep water inside your body, but you've got to replenish that water regularly in order to support your body's most essential needs. Bodies need water to conduct every biological function. Many people experience poor digestion, sluggish thinking, and fatigue because of a lack of clean, pure water. Water is one of the secrets to beautiful skin, in part because it helps eliminate waste from the body and thus removes a burden from the skin.

I recommend that you keep a bottle or a cup of pure water on your desk and sip it throughout the day. Put a bottle of pure spring water on your nightstand and drink when you wake up in the middle of the night feeling parched and thirsty.

The amount of water you drink depends on how your body responds to the water during your first few sips. Sometimes I drink a little water and find myself satisfied. I don't want any more, so I stop. But often I drink a few sips and my entire body awakens to its thirst and need for pure, clean water.

Whenever we are under stress or hurrying through our day, we often become unconscious of our thirst and our need for water. In order to give the body all the water it needs, we must deliberately make a habit of drinking water.

The Middle Region

The area from the eyebrows down to the bottom of the nose reflects the rhythmic system and related organs. In general, the cheeks show the condition of the lungs. Healthy lungs often correspond to clear cheeks that have a bright, vital appearance. Conversely, gray or sallow skin in the area of the cheeks corresponds to lung congestion and low oxygen content. Smokers often have dark pigment in the cheeks. People of all ethnic backgrounds who smoke or eat a high-fat diet often have cheeks that are heavily lined and concave, as if the cheeks were collapsing on themselves. This indicates that the lungs are congested with carbon and fatty deposits and that the oxygen-absorbing capacity of the lungs is low. Acne and other blemishes on the cheeks reveal excesses of fat and sugar in the lungs.

In order to improve the circulation and oxygen content of the lungs, do the following:

* Stop smoking.

* Reduce or eliminate greasy and fatty foods, as well as those containing partially hydrogenated oils such as margarine, high-fat bakery products, and processed foods. A high-fat diet is associated with increased risk of disorders affecting the lungs, including lung cancer.

* Eat more green and leafy vegetables, especially cruciferous vegetables such as broccoli, Brussels sprouts, collard greens, kale, mustard greens, and watercress. Scientific studies associate consumption of these vegetables with lower rates of lung disease. Traditional healers use these vegetables to restore the health of the lungs.

* Walk daily to expel toxins from the lungs and increase oxygen intake.

The area below the eyes, often referred to as the *eyebags,* is associated with the health of the kidneys. The skin at this part of the face is the thinnest and closest to the bone; it therefore reacts more visibly than any other part of the body to swelling and edema. Swelling occurs when the kidneys are weak or tired and unable to adequately regulate the liquid content of the body.

Interestingly, the eyebags do not become swollen from drinking pure water but rather from consuming other liquids that stress the kidneys, such as coffee, soda, and alcohol.

Here's an interesting experiment to try. Examine the region below your eyes carefully. Notice how lined and swollen the skin is. Now, stop drinking coffee, soda, and alcohol for one week and see what effect, if any, this has on your eyebags. Most people witness a tremendous change in this part of the face. The area below the eyes becomes far less lined and

above Clear cheeks that have a bright, vital appearance often correspond to healthy lungs.

swollen. The skin tightens and becomes more youthful. You can substitute black or green tea for coffee and still notice a tremendous improvement. If you get more rest and at least six hours of sleep each night, your eye-bags will likely shrink even further.

To improve the health of the kidneys, do the following:

- Reduce animal protein. Animal protein is converted to uric acid, which taxes the kidneys.

- Eat beans and bean products, such as tempeh and tofu. These foods provide protein in a form that is much more supportive to kidney health than meat is.

- Avoid salt, sugar, caffeine, soft drinks, and alcohol, all of which weaken the kidneys.

The bulb of the nose has long been associated with the health of the heart. The nose can be considered the gateway to the cardiopulmonary system. A swollen or red nose indicates a heart that is expanded and overworked. Excess consumption of fat and alcohol injure the heart and the coronary arteries, the vessels that bring blood and oxygen to the heart. Reduce fatty foods and alcohol, and your cholesterol level will fall significantly. The heart will receive more blood and oxygen, which will improve its health and reduce the redness and swelling of the nose.

To improve the health of the heart, do the following:

- Reduce red meat and dairy foods in order to lower saturated fat consumption. Saturated fat is converted in the body to blood cholesterol, which, when high, is a primary risk factor in heart attack and stroke.

- Avoid processed foods, which commonly contain trans fatty acids, the form of fat most dangerous to the heart.

- Eat high-fiber whole grains, fresh vegetables, and fruits, all of which reduce cholesterol and inflammation in the coronary arteries and lower your risk of heart disease.

- Walk daily, especially in nature.

- Avoid overexerting yourself.

- Reduce and control stress.

- Listen to comforting and nurturing music as often as possible.

below In traditional Chinese medicine, the nose is associated with heart health.

left Rose ingredients are often used in skin care to reduce redness.

The Lower Region

The area of the face from the nose to the chin indicates the health of the digestive tract and reproductive organs.

The digestive system can be considered a long tube that starts at the mouth and ends at the anus. Traditional healers have developed a complex system of understanding the condition of the lips to see the health of the small intestine, large intestine, duodenum (the entrance to the small intestine), and spleen.

In general, the bottom lip corresponds to the large intestine. A swollen bottom lip indicates that the large intestine is itself swollen and lacking in vitality. The upper lip corresponds to the small intestine. A swollen upper lip suggests a swollen small intestine, caused by congestion with fat.

The intestines are healed by following the recommendations described in chapter 3. Be sure to eat more cooked whole grains and cooked vegetables, especially roots (carrots, parsnips, daikon radish, and turnips), and green and leafy vegetables.

Just above the upper lip is the philtrum, a vertical indentation that corresponds with the uterus in women and the prostate in men. In health, the inner area of the philtrum is clear. However, blemishes, swollen tissue, or lines, either vertical or horizontal, within or across the philtrum indicate stagnation and accumulation of fat and toxins in the uterus or prostate. Hormones may also be imbalanced. In women, these blemishes, swellings, and lines often disappear after their menstrual period ends, but if they persist, the stagnation is chronic and accumulating.

The chin also reflects the health of the reproductive organs in both sexes. When the chin is darker than the rest of the face, it suggests stagnation of blood and fat deposits in the reproductive organs. In women, chins that are dark or have mottled skin indicate the possible presence of fibroid tumors. In men, they suggest swelling of the prostate. Boils, blemishes, and moles on the chin or around the mouth indicate accumulation of fat and hormonal imbalances within the reproductive organs.

In general, the chin reflects the strength of our willpower and determination. People with large or prominent chins—Jay Leno comes to mind—have strong willpower and are typically very practical and grounded. They are usually good businesspeople as well. Cleft chins—or a dimple in the chin, like Kirk Douglas's—indicate a passionate nature and a strong constitution.

Restoring the Vitality of the Muscles of the Face

The muscles of the face can be exercised and toned like any other muscle group can. Here are eight exercises that can tighten, tone, and lift your face without your getting near the plastic surgeon's knife.

Exercise 1. The Forehead

These exercises will lift the eyelids and eyebrows and smooth the skin of the forehead. Do this exercise when you see wrinkles on your forehead. It activates the scalp and also slows hair loss.

Place both hands, one over the other, on the forehead, and move the skin of the forehead up and down. As you do the exercise, make sure that the entire scalp moves back and forth as you move the forehead.

Resistance

Smooth the forehead. Place the left hand on the scalp, with the pinkie covering the hairline. Place the pointer and the middle finger of the right hand over the eyebrows and try to lift the eyebrows up with your facial muscles. Your fingers provide resistance to the facial muscles' efforts that lift the eyebrows.

Relaxation

Place the fingertips on the muscles of the forehead and apply light pressure. Shake the head gently with horizontal movements to loosen the muscles.

Exercise 2. The Frown

Do this exercise to lighten the deep lines of the forehead between the eyebrows, at the very top of the nose.

Pull the eyebrows tightly together with your forehead muscles, as you would during deep concentrated reflection.

Lay the middle and ring fingertips of each hand on the outer sides of the eyebrows with a little pressure. Lightly pull the eyebrows toward the outside with your fingers as you gently pull the eyebrows together with your facial muscles against the resistance provided by your fingers.

Relaxation

Consciously relax your face and eyebrows with closed eyes; loosen the muscles by light vibration of the fingertips.

Exercise 3. Shaping the Lower Face (the Chewing Muscle)

Do this exercise to shape the side profile of the cheeks. It lifts the area of the cheeks and brings a youthful and harmonious form to the face.

Clench the back teeth lightly for 1 to 2 minutes. As you clench, increase the pressure slowly, feeling the muscles at the sides of the face contract powerfully.

Resistance

Susan Cudnohufsky is a Bothmer gymnast, an esthetician trainer, and a grandmother of four.

Open the mouth wide, lower the bottom jaw as far as possible, and place an index finger on the bottom row of teeth. Now try to close the mouth while applying pressure to the bottom row of teeth. Allow the index finger to prevent the teeth from closing.

Relaxation

Bend the head slightly forward, open the mouth a bit, and slowly move the head to the left and to the right in a relaxed manner, as if you were saying no.

Exercise 4. Shaping the Floor of the Mouth (the Sterno-hyoidius Muscle)

This is an effective exercise for reducing double chins and improving the profile.

Hold the head upright and tighten the shoulder muscles by moving them slightly back. Roll your tongue back by placing the bottom of the tongue against the upper palate, and push the tip of the tongue backward toward the throat. Now try to swallow. The sterno-hyoidius muscles of the chin will be lifted powerfully. A curvature facing the top of the head is formed under the chin, which causes the double chin to disappear. Repeat the swallowing movement 3 to 5 times.

Variations

1. Attempt to touch the top of the nose with the tongue.
2. Mimic an intensive sucking action, as though you are trying to suck out the contents of an ampule.

Relaxation

Bend the head slightly forward, open the mouth a bit, and slowly move the head to the left and to the right in a relaxed manner, as if you were saying no.

Exercise 5. Shaping the Front Area of the Throat (the Neck Muscles)

This exercise strengthens the circulation of the facial area, firms and rejuvenates the throat, and lifts the breast tissue.

Gently tip the head backward toward the neck. Push the chin forward loosely. Move the lower jaw over the upper jaw while exhaling the remaining air from the chest. Then, with the same chin position, turn the head alternately over the right and then the left shoulder. Look proudly over the shoulders. Repeat the exercise 3 to 5 times.

Resistance

Place your hand around your neck and feel the neck muscles. Now repeat the exercise as described above as you offer mild resistance with your fingers.

Relaxation

Let the head drop loosely forward and backward.

Exercise 6. Shaping the Lateral Throat and Neck Area (the Trapezius Muscles)

This exercise beautifies the neck area. It also strengthens the circulation of the shoulders and back.

Stretch your arms to the sides at shoulder height. Now make forward circular movements, like a bird flying. Start with small circles and continuously increase the size of the circles. Do this for about 2 minutes and then reverse the motion of your arms, making backward circles. Again, gradually increase the size of the circles. Do this for about 2 minutes.

Variation

In an upright posture with the arms hanging, roll the shoulders backward and forward. Do the rolling motions for 3 minutes in the forward direction and then 3 minutes in the backward direction. This exercise reduces fatty deposits on the breasts and loosens the whole throat and neck area.

Relaxation

Let the body slouch forward in a relaxed manner at about a 15-degree angle. Allow the arms to hang down in a relaxed manner. Breathe in and out rhythmically for 2 or 3 minutes.

Your face is a gateway into your inner life. By treating your face with love, compassion, and care, you send those same healing energies into your inner world, where they can work to soothe and heal.

Your face, more than any other part of your body, reveals the quality of your inner life.

Chapter 5

Healing Specific Skin Conditions

Virtually all common skin disorders fall within five categories. At Dr. Hauschka, we regard these skin types as temporary conditions, not permanent states. Each can be healed if it is treated in the right way. The five most common skin conditions are as follows:

Oily skin is caused when the skin becomes hyperactive. Cellular renewal speeds up and sebaceous glands become overactive, leading to the overproduction of oils and sebum. Among the consequences of overactive, oily skin are excess oil at the surface of the skin, pimples, blemishes, boils, acne, inflammation, and scarring.

Dry skin occurs when the normal maintenance and rejuvenating functions of the skin go to sleep. The skin stops moisturizing itself and the sebaceous glands become lazy, producing less sebum. The epidermis is also often weak, allowing the moisture below to come to the surface and evaporate. The result is dry, chapped, and flaky skin that can peel away in tiny bits. The skin is literally dehydrated and needs the right kind of support.

Perhaps, surprisingly, dry skin frequently arises when we become addicted to moisturizers that replace the normal functions of the skin. Like bones, muscles, and organs, the skin must be allowed to work in order to function properly. Prevent a person from exercising and his muscles and bones atrophy. Overload the skin with moisturizers and synthetic skin care products and the skin's natural moisturizing and healing functions likewise atrophy.

Other factors that cause dry skin are overexposure to sunlight, air-conditioning, or indoor heating; environmental pollution; the use of harsh exfoliates and synthetic skin care products; and not drinking enough water. The skin needs to be healed, especially the epidermal layer, which protects the skin's moisture content.

Sensitive skin comes in two types. The first is redness caused by too much blood flowing to a specific area of the body or face. Capillaries expand and often open to the air. Factors that either cause or exacerbate such redness are exhaustion, stress, excess consumption of spicy foods and alcohol, and changes in temperature and climate. Rosacea is among the most common manifestations of this type of sensitivity.

The second arises when the skin becomes flaky and itchy and develops spots of redness. Such a condition can emerge from emotional distress, changes in climate and temperature, and travel.

Aging skin is accelerated when we are overexposed to free radicals, which are caused primarily by cigarette smoking, exposure to sunlight, industrial and environmental pollutants, a diet rich in processed and animal foods, and prolonged stress.

Normal skin is a result of the skin's basic functions of self-moisturizing, healing, renewal, and cleansing working in a balanced and optimal way. Most people with normal skin also experience periods when one part of the skin is slightly oily while another part is dry. This is referred to as *combination skin.*

The skin, remarkably, is constantly healing itself. Given the right conditions—such as a healing diet, exercise, and healing external treatments—it can restore much of its beauty and inspiring glow. All the skin care recommendations provided address all five skin conditions. In fact, if you follow the dietary and skin care advice described in the preceding chapters, most skin disorders will clear up by themselves.

Nevertheless, some intractable conditions call for further care. The following homemade treatments use medicinal plants or herbs to treat acne and rosacea. Follow with homemade moisturizers to treat dry skin and homemade toners to treat oily and normal skin.

Alternatively, use a variety of Dr. Hauschka products for all five types of skin conditions.

A Healing Mask for Acne

Combine 1 teaspoon each of the following ingredients: honey, wheat germ, and goldenseal powder. Mix thoroughly and apply to your face for 10 minutes. Apply the mask twice a week.

Herbal Formula for Treating Rosacea

Cleanse your face with a homemade oatmeal soap.

Fill a quart-sized basin with water and add $1/2$ cup rolled or steel-cut oats. Mix gently until the water becomes cloudy. Allow 5 to 10 minutes for the oats to settle to the bottom of the basin. Gently and lovingly rinse your face with just the oatmeal water. Avoid applying the actual grain to your face. Use the press-and-roll motion described in chapter 4 to cleanse.

After cleansing, apply a homemade toner that contains any or all of the following herbs: goldenseal, yarrow, and chamomile. (Instructions for making the toner are described on page 75.)

Herbal Formula for Treating Acne

Virtually all traditional herbalists begin their treatment of acne by supporting and strengthening the blood-cleansing organs, especially the liver and kidneys. The process begins, of course, by eliminating foods that burden these organs, especially those that are processed or contain caffeine, sugar, artificial substances, pesticides, and high levels of fat.

The following herbal formula reduces the burden on blood-cleansing organs and supports the elimination of acne.

Combine 1 teaspoon each of the following dried herbs in 4 to 5 cups of water: burdock root, dandelion root, gingerroot, nettles herb, Oregon grape root, red root, and yellow dock. Boil for 10 minutes. Remove from the heat and allow the brew to steep for 10 minutes. Drink 1 cup twice a day for three days straight, and then abstain from the formula for three days. These six days are considered a single round. Repeat for three to four more rounds.

At the same time, use the recommended herbal cleansers, moisturizers, and toners, the toner preferably containing echinacea.

Healing Skin, the Dr. Hauschka Way

Rudolf Hauschka and Elisabeth Sigmund applied Rudolf Steiner's threefold approach to create skin care products that address specific problems in specific areas of the body. In general, plants have a threefold nature like that of humans. The roots of plants are where the nutrients are absorbed. The plant's stem and leaves provide respiratory, circulatory, and elimination functions, which are rhythmic in nature. The flower, seeds, and fruit correspond to reproduction and metabolism. By using corresponding parts of the medicinal plant, Hauschka and Sigmund targeted specific parts of the body.

When she joined forces with Dr. Hauschka, Sigmund began applying this three-fold understanding to every type of skin condition with tremendous success. Here are the Dr. Hauschka approaches to each condition.

Oily Skin: Sluggish in One Part, Overactive in Another

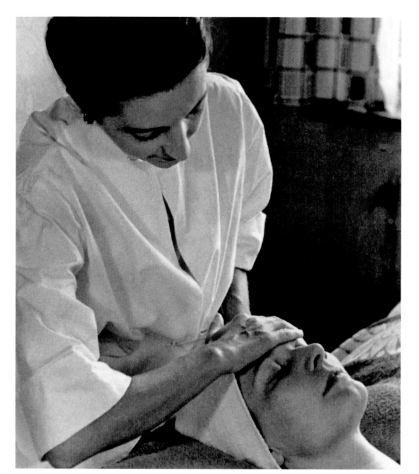

Oily skin occurs when the sebaceous glands become overactive and produce too much sebum, or what we perceive as oil on the surface of the skin. There are several possible causes, including heredity, hormones, lifestyle, and a sluggish metabolism.

By applying the Dr. Hauschka understanding, however, we can see more clearly the source of the problem. The digestive tract is sluggish, which causes waste to overburden the lymph system. The waste makes its way to the skin, where the lymph and sebaceous glands work overtime to eliminate the toxins through the pores. In essence, the more sluggish your digestion, the more your skin suffers.

Elisabeth Sigmund successfully applied Rudolf Steiner's threefold understanding to every type of skin condition.

That means we must do all we can to support our digestive function. At the same time, I recommend the following Dr. Hauschka regimen for day and night skin care.

1. Use Dr. Hauschka Cleansing Cream every morning and evening. Wash for three to five minutes each time using the press-and-roll motion described in chapter 4. The Cleansing Cream not only removes dirt and pollution particles but also provides a gentle exfoliation that removes blackheads and waste products that have accumulated in the pores.

2. Follow the Cleansing Cream with Dr. Hauschka Clarifying Toner, which calms, hydrates, tones, and promotes healing of the skin.

3. Complete the morning cleansing by gently pressing a few drops of Normalizing Day Oil into the face. The oil awakens the skin to the fact that there is enough oil to protect its damaged outer covering. That will signal the sebaceous glands to relax and reduce oil production. It also loosens impure congested oils and refines the pores. Gently rub Normalizing Day Oil between the hands and then gently and lovingly press it into the skin.

4. In the evenings, remove face and eye makeup with Dr. Hauschka Cleansing Milk.

5. Apply Rhythmic Night Conditioner for three consecutive twenty-eight-day periods to normalize oily skin.

6. Occasionally use Dr. Hauschka Lemon Bath to awaken and revitalize the skin and restore a youthful brightness. You may also add a drop of Lemon Bath to your cleansing water in cases of extreme oiliness.

Healing Acne

Acne arises when the sebaceous glands become overactive and sebum collects and blocks hair follicles and pores. As the keratinocytes migrate upward from the lower levels of the skin, they get bogged down in the sebum. Soon, these cells die and become trapped in the follicles and pores. The excess sebum and dead cells form a plug, or a blackhead, in the pore, which prevents normal drainage of the oil. As the excess sebum accumulates, bacteria collect in large populations that feed on the sebum. They also cause irritations in the skin and, eventually, infections, which combine to form a pustule, or a pimple.

Other factors come into play. Hormonal imbalances increase the production of sebum, which means more blocked pores and infections that, in turn, create pustules and rashes of acne.

Weak digestion triggers the increased production of sebum. Meanwhile, the kidneys and liver do not filter the higher levels of hormones in the blood, and these

healing specific skin conditions

hormones stimulate sebum production. Thus, improving liver and kidney and digestive function by following the guidance provided above is essential for healthy skin. You can also do a great deal more with appropriate skin care. Here's the Dr. Hauschka regimen for healing acne:

1. Use Dr. Hauschka Cleansing Cream each morning and evening. The gentle exfoliant cleanses and opens pores and allows excess sebum to flow unimpeded.

2. Follow the Cleansing Cream with Dr. Hauschka Clarifying Toner, which completes the cleansing process, tones the skin, and promotes healing.

3. Each morning, use a few drops of Normalizing Day Oil to calm and relax the sebaceous glands while refining pore size. You can combine Normalizing Day Oil with Translucent Bronze Concentrate, which contains plant extracts and plant oils, to heal scarring, even pigmentation, and provide a healthy, sun-kissed glow.

4. At night, use Dr. Hauschka Cleansing Milk to remove makeup.

5. Every evening, cleanse your skin with Cleansing Cream and then apply Clarifying Toner or Rhythmic Night Conditioner.

6. Once a week, use Facial Steam Bath and Cleansing Clay Mask. You can do this two or three times a week if the acne condition is severe.

   Facial Steam Bath, which has antibacterial and antiseptic properties, opens blocked pores and reduces inflammation. Use the Steam Bath for ten to fifteen minutes. Follow with Cleansing Clay Mask, which is made from a finely ground clay and herbal extracts, including nasturtium and witch hazel. Cleansing Clay Mask opens and cleans pores, absorbs and removes secretions, and heals sores.

7. Occasionally add Lemon Bath oils to your cleansing water in the morning. Essential oil of lemon awakens, rejuvenates, and tones the skin, and it is an antiseptic and an antibacterial. Sage bath oil in the evening draws out impurities as well. You can combine essential oil of sage with your evening wash.

You will see an enormous difference in the health and clarity of your skin within a few days, and if you follow this regimen regularly for a few weeks, the results can be amazing.

above In Dr. Hauschka Clarifying Toner, nasturtium calms and soothes overactive skin.

Dry Skin: Awaken the Inner Moisturizers

Dry skin ages more rapidly than moist tissue, which is why we want to heal this problem as quickly as possible. Dry skin arises from a lack of oil production by the sebaceous glands. It's as if the sebaceous glands have become tired and perhaps have fallen to sleep. Age, heredity, hormonal imbalances, smoking, the use of certain drugs, and an unhealthy lifestyle can all lead to dry skin.

In order to properly treat the condition, we must ask if the dryness is accompanied by sensitivity, or outbreaks of a rash or rosacea, or whether the skin is clear despite the dryness.

below Moisture is essential to healthy skin.

left Lemon awakens, rejuvenates, and tones the skin.

For Dryness Without Sensitivity or Rosacea

1. Cleanse the face with Cleansing Cream twice a day. The gentle exfoliation of Cleansing Cream removes dead cells that lie on the skin's surface and stimulates the sebaceous glands. Cleansing Cream may be alternated with Cleansing Milk to remove makeup.

2. Apply Facial Toner after cleansing the face.

3. While the face is still damp from the toner, apply Moisturizing Day Cream, which is an activating moisturizer that encourages oil production in the sebaceous glands. Moisturizing Day Cream, which contains extracts of anthyllis, witch hazel, and Saint-John's-wort, both heals the skin and jump-starts the sebaceous glands, which in turn promotes the skin's own moisturizing mechanisms.

4. In order to seal in the moisturizer and provide extra protection, apply any of the following day creams over your moisturizer: Quince Day Cream, Rose Day Cream, or Toned Day Cream.

5. Apply Rhythmic Night Conditioner after cleansing for two twenty-eight-day periods.

6. Use Moisturizing Mask, which, among other healing ingredients, contains quince, a plant with remarkable moisture-retaining properties. The plant oils in Moisturizing Mask seep deeply into the skin, infusing it with moisture while stimulating the sebaceous glands to resume their moisture-producing activities. This moisturizer also contains the wax from the rose, which gently seals in moisture without blocking the pores and hair follicles.

7. Facial Steam Bath and Rejuvenating Mask can also be used. The latter revitalizes dull, lackluster skin, shrinks enlarged pores and blemishes, and softens hardened skin.

healing specific skin conditions

101

For Dry Skin with Sensitivity or Rosacea

Rosacea is an inflammation of the capillaries within the dermis. The capillaries may become so swollen that they become visible, creating a spidery web of inflamed vessels that are sometimes covered with a thin layer of oil. The most common site is the bulb of the nose, but the condition can appear on other areas of the face. Rosacea usually emerges between the ages of thirty-five and forty-five. Its causes are not well understood, although heredity, diet, specific food sensitivities, alcohol, and lifestyle all can play roles. For many people, sugar, wine, and spicy foods can trigger the condition, or exacerbate it.

The condition can progress to a more acute phase known as *acne rosacea*, which is a combination of blemishes and swollen capillaries.

Here's what you can do to relieve rosacea:

1. Keep a food diary to see if there is any correlation between the condition and specific foods, especially the common offenders listed above. When a correlation is noted, significantly reduce or eliminate the food. In addition to tracking the foods and drinks mentioned above, note the effects of foods that combine sugar and poor-quality fats.

2. Get plenty of rest and deep sleep.

3. Use Cleansing Milk twice a day. Cleansing Milk, which contains witch hazel, fermented grain extracts, and healing plants, is extremely gentle. It contains no exfoliants, which means it soothes rather than irritates the skin.

4. Follow the morning cleansing with Dr. Hauschka Rhythmic Conditioner, Sensitive. This product soothes, calms, and reduces inflamed vessels and tissues. Among its ingredients are extracts from borage (a healing plant), witch hazel, English oak, pearl powder Veronica, chamomile, and rose hip (rich in antioxidants). Rhythmic Conditioner, Sensitive, is calming. It strengthens connective tissue and heals the skin.

5. After cleansing and toning, apply Rose Day Cream moisturizer. Rose Day Cream combines an array of delicate plant oils, including rose petal, rose hip, marshmallow, Saint-John's-wort, and avocado, all of which moisturize and heal sensitive skin and rosacea.

6. Rejuvenating Mask and Firming Mask are excellent treatments.

7. Lavender Bath or Spruce Bath in the cleansing water is soothing.

For Advanced Rosacea

In advanced cases, rosacea becomes even more inflamed and pustules may appear. Use the same regimen described above, but add Lavender Bath Oil to your cleansing water in the morning and at night. During the day, press a couple drops of Normalizing Day Oil into the skin with a drop of Translucent Bronze Concentrate for extra soothing and calming. Rejuvenating Mask can be used periodically at night to reduce inflammation, cleanse the skin, and remove excess oils. Firming Mask can also be used to hydrate and strengthen the connective tissues of the face.

Skin problems prove the rule that the outer affects the inner, and the inner the outer. Anyone who has ever suffered any sort of skin problem, such as acne or rosacea, knows the emotional distress these disorders can cause. The Dr. Hauschka approach to healing beauty can rapidly restore the health and beauty to your skin, no matter what its current condition. First, eat foods and engage in behaviors that can improve the function of your intestines and kidneys. This alone will dramatically improve the health of your skin. At the same time, use the medicinal cleansers, toners, and moisturizers recommended to further heal and enhance your skin's beauty.

Daisy has astringent and anti-inflammatory properties that help calm red, irritated skin.

Chapter 6

Alchemy: Transforming Your Inner and Outer Beauty

Ancient alchemists believed it was possible to turn base metals, such as lead, into gold. Some feel that the true meaning of alchemy is that each of us is attempting to transform our base nature—our lead, you might say—into what the Greeks described as goodness, truth, and beauty, the gold that lies inside us. We've all experienced this alchemical transformation many times. On one day we feel and look downright awful, and the next we are radiant, inside and out. Somehow we managed to turn lead into gold, though most of us are unable to explain just how we did it. The same miracle occurs in healing; we go from being sick and weak to healthy and full of vitality, often without doing anything more than simply resting. How does such a transformation occur, we would like to know, and can we do anything to encourage it?

Dr. Hauschka believed he knew the answer to that question. He agreed with Rudolf Steiner that the physical body is imbued with an underlying energy, a life force, that animates it and sustains its functions. Without this life force, the body is largely a collection of minerals and proteins that quickly decay and return to the earth when the life energy leaves it. As Steiner put it, the only time you see just the physical body is when you see a corpse. At all other times, you are looking at a human being with a physical and spiritual anatomy that has four distinct aspects.

The first dimension is the material, or physical body, the part we can see. The second is the life force, or life energy—what the Chinese refer to as *chi* and what Steiner called the *etheric body*. Your life force is an integrated body of energy that infuses every cell, organ, and system of your body. The etheric energy body determines the vitality and youthfulness of your physical body. A strong etheric body causes your physical body to age more slowly and maintain its youth for a much longer period. The third aspect of your humanity is your emotional body, or what Steiner called the *astral aspect* of your being. This is the part that has distinct likes and dislikes; it reacts to your experiences and plays a central role in your decisions and behaviors. The fourth is your spirit. Steiner said that this spiritual aspect of your being understands your purpose for living. It also lives on after your physical body dies. Steiner maintained that, in the end, all of us are attempting to infuse the physical, etheric, and emotional planes with the spiritual dimension of our lives—a transformation that, among other things, brings about greater goodness, truth, and beauty.

The way to restore health and enhance your beauty, however, is to infuse your body with an abundance of life energy, Hauschka and Steiner said. This enhanced life energy elevates the function of all your organs and systems. It brings your emotions into balance and promotes feelings of confidence, well-being, and joy. It imbues your physical body with harmony and radiance that emerges as true beauty.

Dr. Hauschka dedicated his life to developing plant-based medicines that contain both the plant's active ingredients and its life energies. In the 1920s, he created a seven-day rhythmical process in which he used the opposing forces of nature—light and darkness, coolness and warmth, motion and stillness—to coax forth the medicinal ingredients and vital energies from the plant so they could be administered to people. He and Elisabeth Sigmund brought this same approach to the Dr. Hauschka Skin Care Products.

In our own way, each of us is searching for ways to boost our life force and enjoy the fruits that such an experience brings. There are many ways to do that, and all of them contribute to making you healthier and more beautiful.

Dr. Hauschka's unique extraction methods preserve the vital energies of living plants.

Boosting Your Life Force for Health and Beauty

Everyone who touches you with caring, compassion, or love elevates your life energy and contributes to your health and beauty. The opposite is also true. Touching a person in anger or with selfishness weakens the life force. Your body can sense what's in the heart of the person whose touch it feels. Sometimes the body welcomes that touch—indeed, it can drink up the energy that passes from the person who offers a loving or healing touch. At other times, the body recoils from or armors itself against negative feelings implicit in a person's touch.

We all seek to be touched with love or caring because these are the mediums through which an abundance of life energy can pass between people. A loving or caring touch has the potential to raise our life energy, improve our health, and enhance our beauty.

All forms of skin and body care enhance your life force and boost your health and beauty—that is, when they are administered by someone who is loving, compassionate, and skilled. A facial given by such a person can transform you. So, too, can a therapeutic massage. The esthetician's or the healer's skill and compassion are transmitted from her hands into your skin and etheric body, making your etheric field stronger and more alive. The result is a dramatic change on every level of your being—your mood is softer and more balanced; your body is more in harmony and therefore healthier; and your appearance is more relaxed, open, and beautiful.

Rudolf Steiner described in great detail the energetic connection between people. Our thoughts, emotions, and words are bundles of etheric energy, Steiner said, that pass from one person to the next. That same etheric energy passes between people when they touch. The effects thoughts, emotions, words, and touch have on us depend on the type of emotion and intention they carry. For example, Steiner said that loving thoughts, intended to support other human beings, take a form similar to a flower. When you think loving or caring thoughts about another person, bundles of etheric energy leave your body and enter the field of the person for whom they are intended. There they enrich, strengthen, and brighten the person's etheric body, overall health, and beauty.

Each of us creates our reality on the basis of our thoughts, emotions, and actions. On the other hand, our inner realities are also created by the types of etheric energies to which we are exposed. This gives us a tremendous power to strengthen our health, improve our lives, and develop our beauty. We can do this simply by exposing ourselves to many sources of love, compassion, and care. All of the following practices do exactly that.

- Spend time in nature. A forest is packed with harmonious etheric energy. The ocean sends waves upon waves of beautiful life force to you. Nature literally bathes us in life energy, which is why we feel so different after we've

spent a little time by the sea or in a wood. The etheric waves are creating order, harmony, and beauty inside you. A thirty-minute walk in a park or a wood or by a river, a lake, or the sea has the power to transform your inner world and outer beauty.

Here's a little experiment you can do. Take a quiet half-hour walk with a friend by a lake, along the ocean, or in a forest. Before you take such a walk, take a good look at your friend's face. Notice the expression and the lines on her or his face. After the walk, again look closely at your friend's face. In the vast majority of cases, you will notice that your friend has relaxed. His or her face will be fuller, more alive, and less lined. He or she will look younger. The effect will not simply be in his or her appearance, however. You both will feel more vital, more alive, and more balanced emotionally. You have been profoundly changed by the harmony and beauty of nature and thus become more harmonious and beautiful yourself.

If possible, spend thirty minutes a week walking in nature.

- Eat unprocessed plant foods, especially fresh vegetables, fruits, and whole grains that have been grown biodynamically or organically. Fresh foods that have been grown in clean, pure soil retain their life energies even after harvest. Those life energies infuse your body when you eat these foods. Steiner said that we need the forces of all vital foods to develop a strong, healthy spiritual life.

- Express gratitude and love throughout the day, especially when you drink water or when you bathe or shower. Whenever you drink water, consider expressing love and gratitude silently into the water before you drink. Do the same when you bathe or shower.

In chapter 1, I suggested you "potentize" your bath water by swirling the water in the shape of a figure 8. As you do this, express your gratitude for your beautiful body and your life. Express the love you have for your life, for yourself, and for those closest to you. These thoughts will enter the water and promote your health and beauty as you bathe.

- Dance or do rhythmic exercise. *Eurythmy,* a form of therapeutic dance based on Steiner's teachings, blends harmonious movements to strengthen your etheric body, overall health, and beauty. All forms of rhythmic dance, such as ballroom or tango, boost life energy. So, too, do rhythmic forms of exercise such as tai chi chuan, chi gong, yoga, and tennis.

- Seek out therapeutic massage and healing touch, including Reiki and massage practices founded on the ancient Chinese practice of acupuncture. Acupuncture is a 3,000-year-old healing art based on the perception that life energy flows through the physical body along distinct pathways, or meridians. Along these meridians lie hundreds of acupuncture points that when stimulated by the shallow insertion of a needle or by pressure

from the practitioner's fingers act as generators of life energy. Many scientists have used sensitive electronic equipment to demonstrate that these points do indeed trigger an electrical charge that runs along the meridian lines described by Chinese healers.

- Listen to beautiful, harmonious music. As everyone knows, music can change our life condition in seconds. Music, of course, is harmonious waves of energy that transform your physical, etheric, and emotional bodies, thus restoring inner balance and beauty to your life. Try to hear live music whenever possible. Local colleges and universities are good places to hear all kinds of music, from classical to jazz, folk, and rock and roll.

- Use skin care products made of pure plant substances, preferably grown biodynamically or organically.

- Practice rhythm. Your health and beauty depend on your capacity to create and sustain an orderly life.

All of these practices will strengthen your etheric energy, which in turn will support your physical, emotional, and spiritual health and beauty. Everything that supports your life force also promotes the health, youthfulness, and beauty of your skin. These life-supporting activities are therefore practical forms of skin care.

Still, aging is inevitable, which means we must become more and more conscious of exposing ourselves to the sources of healing and beauty. As we age, we must become wise. You don't need to know very much at twenty or twenty-five in order to look young and be beautiful. But when you start passing through your thirties, forties, and fifties, your health and beauty increasingly depend on the wisdom of your choices and how well you care for yourself.

There's a reason for that, Steiner said. During your mid-thirties, the life force turns its attention away from your physical body and toward your internal development, namely your wisdom and spiritual growth. The universe has a plan for you, Steiner said, and it is written into all four levels of your being. That plan unfolds in its own unique way so that you can become fulfilled and truly beautiful—that is, unless you fight it.

Embrace and Make the Most of the Stage of Life You Are In

Our culture is waging war against the natural and inevitable process of aging. In messages that are all too obvious, the culture draws a line in the sand, so to speak, and says that after the age of thirty-five, we are increasingly uninteresting and less and less beautiful. All that is good, true, and beautiful in our mature years is often dismissed or ignored. The consequence is that we know little about the aging process, and even less about the gifts that await us after the age of forty.

Every ancient and traditional culture has offered a kind of mythological blueprint for how humans develop, become their own unique selves, and fulfill their purpose for living. This blueprint was intended to reveal the challenges, rewards, and potential beauty in each stage of life. There are rewards and gifts to be earned and integrated at each phase of your maturity. Every one of those gifts is essential if you are to become whole and fulfilled.

Rudolf Steiner observed that human life unfolds in seven-year cycles. He maintained that in your mid-thirties, your life force makes a dramatic turn away from the physical body. At that point, it devotes itself increasingly to the job of developing your inner world and your spiritual life. As you age, less and less energy is dedicated to keeping young, while more and more is used to develop your growing wisdom and spiritual connection to the universe at large.

From ages 7 to 14 we have strong physical health and an abundance of energy.

Ages 0 to 7:
Coming into Life

The first seven years of life are a gradual development into individuality. The child's energetic, or etheric, body is still strongly linked to its mother, especially in the first few years. During these early years, it's impossible for the child to distinguish between herself and her mother.

Our conventional way of thinking is to picture us as growing up after birth, but Steiner maintained that we, in effect, "grow down." What he meant was that the etheric, emotional, and spiritual aspects of our nature gradually join with the physical body, and as they do, we develop individuality.

The first sign of that individuality is the development of mobility: crawling, and then walking. Slowly, we come to know more and more about what we want and need. We develop preferences and temperament. All of this suggests that more and more of who we truly are is grounded in physical form.

When the life force is sufficiently grounded in the body, the child's energetic body is strong enough to cause the teeth to burst forth, which gives him or her the ability to eat solid food. At about five years of age, the child goes off to school, and not long afterward, perhaps at six or seven, permanent teeth appear. We have gradually moved away from the mother and into greater and greater stages of individuality. We are now ready for the next phase of our maturity.

Ages 7 to 14:
Stronger Health and Healing Abilities

Between the ages of seven and fourteen, childhood illnesses can appear, such as measles, mumps, and chicken pox. This is the moment when the immune system must become strong in order to give us the defenses we need to survive. High fevers develop, the body fights for its health and life, and in the process, the immune system arises as a powerful ally that can ward off antagonists from the environment. At the same time, hormones change and the body rapidly matures.

In order for the immune system to meet the challenges of the environment, the etheric body must be fully grounded in the physical body. The body needs all of its energies to fight off illness. Therefore, it draws the life force to itself. The etheric body fully joins the physical body. Once the childhood diseases are overcome, the energy from the life force is used to fuel a rapid burst of hormonal and physical changes. We have strong physical health and an abundance of energy, and we're ready to enter the next big stage in life—puberty and the ability to procreate.

Ages 14 to 21:
The Emotional Realm Comes into Being

The next phase of life is characterized by the incarnation of the emotional body, or what Steiner called the *astral body*. Emotions become turbulent and control most of our actions. In fact, the entire period is dominated by the emotional aspect of our humanity. We fall in love; we fall out of love; we create close relationships and break up relationships. We are overcome by our instincts and emotional needs. The rational faculties are not fully grounded as yet, and consequently the emotional drives are difficult, if not impossible, to harness. Steiner maintained that we are very much in our animal nature during this period, which is why we can make enormous mistakes. We are driven by forces that we don't necessarily understand.

Ages 21 to 28:
Play That Turns Toward Responsibility

While the early part of this period is characterized by independence, enthusiasm, and play—often with wild abandon—an underlying movement pushes us to become more responsible for our actions. Youthful vitality and health are so strong for most people during this period that we rarely, if ever, consider our health or physical vulnerability. Many believe there is infinite time ahead, which further encourages them to play. But even as these forces drive us, an underlying current is asking us to wake up to the consequences of our actions and to become responsible adults.

Many women and men are rapidly brought down to earth by the arrival of children, a life-altering event (or series of events) that requires us to be more responsible and less selfish. Our wild years give way to sacrifice for our spouse and family.

During this period, we become more aware of our natural talents and abilities. The true, spiritual nature has descended deeply enough for us to have some inkling of our special characteristics and how we can utilize them to support our lives.

In effect, this is a period in which we are gradually "landing," and as we do, we grow in our awareness of our talents and responsibilities. Steiner said this period can be characterized by the centaur, the mythological animal that is half-human and half-horse. The human is now rising out of the animal nature. We are still driven by our instincts and desires but are becoming more and more aware of our humanity and our unique characteristics. We are also becoming more aware of what we came into life to do.

Ages 28 to 35: Peaking

During these years, our physical and intellectual powers are peaking. Interestingly, the skeleton reaches its greatest density and strength at this point. After thirty-five, most people begin losing bone mass at a rate of about 1 percent per year. The skeleton is a metaphor for our physical powers and connection to the earth, which also have reached their apex. We are now at the point when we are most deeply rooted in life and in the world. For most of us, our talents have announced themselves; we have found our professions. We are fully engaged in the struggle to get ahead and to achieve our earthly ambitions. We tend to be highly competitive, and it is not uncommon to compete with others for position or status. We want to be the best at whatever we are doing.

During this period, we are also sponges for knowledge. We read, study, and pursue intellectual topics for the sheer pleasure of learning. Very often, our studies are in some area that holds special significance to us. This effort may endure as a hobby for many years to come or eventually blossom into a profession.

We are fully in charge of our physical powers and instincts and use them for our personal ambitions.

Ages 35 to 42: A Time of Challenge and Crisis

Just when things are going well and continual expansion seems the natural course of things, the party balloons pop. Disappointment occurs—and sometimes, crisis. Many get divorced; others experience a financial or health crisis. We are forced to question our direction, values, and patterns of behavior. We're no longer so sure or confident. We see our limitations and turn inward.

The current is leading us away from a materialistic view of life. Though the crises tend to occur closer to forty-two than to thirty-five, the trend is clearly away from a narrow focus on our ambitions. The spirit is now fully grounded within us and starting to influence our thinking. This is just the beginning, but our priorities are starting to change.

Steiner's image is of the man or woman now leading the horse by the reins. Our humanity is in front of our instincts. We have begun to search in places where instincts alone cannot lead. The spirit is just starting to take over the leadership of our lives. But because this is a time of transition from purely materialistic values to those influences led by spirit, we tend to be more confused than certain about our direction.

Ages 42 to 49: Effectiveness on Earth

As we move closer to forty-nine, we see our children go off and become independent (or at least less dependent on us). This frees us from many of our old responsibilities and causes us to examine what we want to do with the rest of our lives. Many women begin to experience perimenopause, or the first hints that hormonal changes are occurring and that physical fertility is waning. There is a period of soul-searching and of wonder. Whether we acknowledge it or not, we naturally turn toward spirituality for answers.

This is a period during which we are blessed with growing creativity and imagination, which helps us set off in a new direction or create a new professional life. For those already established in professions, imagination helps us achieve even more, without struggling as hard as was necessary before. A certain mastery begins to emerge. We are more relaxed and at peace, both in ourselves and with the world around us. We start to mellow. Those who were temperamental or intense start to soften and become more gentle.

Meanwhile, we develop a broader, more humanitarian vision of life. We see our connections to others, even those at a great distance. We care about conditions within our community, our country, and the world. We want to be of service to others. We see service as a way of giving meaning to our lives. These are all values of spirit, which increasingly call on us to grow and see the oneness of life.

Steiner called this period the arrival of spirit-man or spirit-woman. It is a time when the soul has gained control of our lives and imposes its values upon us. We begin to see, if only intuitively, that a balance must be achieved between our earthly needs and our idealistic concerns for humanity. As we move closer to forty-nine, we start to see those parts of our lives we overemphasized and those parts we did not value sufficiently. This is a time of self-reflection.

After forty-two, our intuition becomes stronger. Increasingly, our intuitive powers, which Steiner referred to as arising from a spiritual source, become our compass in life.

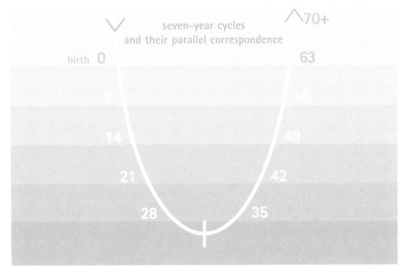

Rudolf Steiner observed that human life unfolds in seven-year cycles.

Ages 49 to 56: A Growing Vision and Understanding of Life

Just as imagination was the gift in our forties, inspiration becomes the gift of our fifties. Most women have experienced menopause by now, which completes the journey from physical fertility and preoccupation with one's own children to greater freedom and a growing desire to serve the human family. Women and men alike find themselves taking ever more powerful roles at their jobs, in their communities, and in society. This is the time when our experience and knowledge of how to get things done can be combined with our ideals and broad vision of life. This should be a time of mastery and power. After you turn fifty, people begin to take you seriously. Your experience and wisdom give you a certain gravitas that convey power and authority. As long as you have taken good care of your health, you can now become the person you have always longed to be. You are blessed with a second wind that can take you the rest of the way in your life. The dream of being your true self takes shape. It is within your grasp.

Those who have neglected their spiritual life feel increasingly confused by aging. They are also terrified of mortality. They cling to an illusory and faded youth.

Ages 56 to 63: The Crossroads—Mastery or Reevaluation

Fifty-six is a major turning point in life, Steiner said. If you have allowed your true inner nature to manifest and guide you, you may be blessed with tremendous intuitive powers. Your intuition has now developed to such a degree that you have a clear sense of where to go and what to do. You are guided by an inner knowledge that helps you use your energy much more efficiently. Your inner knowledge also serves as a great source of comfort. You feel protected and inspired by a sense of purpose and direction. Your spirit has given you a task to perform. That task is the core of your work and your reason for being.

At the same time, you are more relaxed and at peace than at any other time in your life. You no longer feel much inner conflict and have few outer conflicts. As long as you have cared for your health and retain your vitality, you are able to enjoy your life without the same degree of worry or fear. Problems that caused you great upset in the past seem like minor disturbances, little more than irritations in the grand scheme of your life. Time slows during this period. You're not in a great rush, though you seem to get more accomplished with less effort. You are at the peak of your powers, making this a time of reward and achievement.

On the other hand, if you have lived a materialistic life and have denied the spiritual influences within you, you may experience a life-altering crisis around the ages of fifty-six to fifty-eight. Loss of direction, career crisis, serious illness, the breakup of a relationship, or the terror of mortality all can wreak havoc on your psyche. You may look back on your life with terrible regret. Mistakes made in youth—especially those that caused others pain—seem even larger now than they did at the time. All of this can bring about a spiritual crisis that if addressed with care and compassion, can bring a spiritual renewal and a new direction in life.

Ages 63 to 70: A Time of Harvesting and Spreading the Wealth

This is a time of blessing, grace, and opportunity. In traditional communities, people of this age were the elders, those who were turned to for their wisdom, vision, and intuitive gifts. We have been freed from the struggles of life, yet we may still have considerable energy and vitality. We are teachers, advisors, guides, and sources of inspiration to others. This is the period when we wish to give back to those who come after us and are still embroiled in the struggles of life. It is a time of great power and reward. We still care deeply about the struggles of others, yet we are no longer bound by those struggles ourselves. Our main tether to society is our love and caring and the knowledge that others still need the gift of our experience, wisdom, and guidance.

Ages 70 and Beyond: Reflection

This is a time for you. This period is about taking stock of your life, reflecting on the past, and experiencing the richness of the present. You are at the threshold of rebirth into the next world, and you are preparing yourself for that next adventure. You are awaiting the call.

There are blessings and beauty to be experienced at every stage of life, but for those who allow life to unfold in its natural order, the blessings become richer and ever more beautiful as they mature. As a culture, we have emphasized the first half of life, especially the period from the teenage years to age thirty-five. We have failed to understand the second half of life, which may be the source of the journey's greatest gifts and most rewarding joys. But those who embrace maturity and find its gifts look back on youth with compassion and a certain sympathy. The real beauty of life does not appear to us until we have personally experienced the underlying forces of love and generosity that attempt to bring each of us to fulfillment.

Chapter 7

Practicing Beauty

As you now know, practicing beauty is about practicing self-love. As discussed in chapter 1, many of us are constantly giving of ourselves, partly because our schedules are shaped by the needs of others. That means our schedules need some tweaking, you might say. To be more specific, we need to find more time for ourselves. Those who say, "There is no time for me" are committed to self-sacrifice, which has its own rewards, but none as joyful as the pleasure of a good bath or a wonderful massage—both of which can be accomplished in thirty minutes or less.

The benefits of the Practicing Beauty Program can affect every area of your life. You will be amazed at how different you will feel about yourself and those around you when you spend just a little more time taking care of yourself. Some of the positive effects that flow from this program are more beautiful skin, greater relaxation, higher self-esteem, a feeling that you are more in control of your life, less stress and fear, more vitality, and far better overall health.

The Program

Practicing Beauty is a twelve-step program that is carried out over a thirty-day period. At the end of that period, you will very likely find that nearly every area of your life has been positively affected. You do not have to adopt all twelve to benefit from the program. However, try to adopt as many of the recommendations as you can for the simple reason that the more steps you adopt, the greater the overall benefit. Let's start with some guidelines.

Quality Determines Quantity

The quality of a skin care product, or a food, determines its effects on your skin, health, and happiness. Most of our health problems today, especially obesity, come from two related sources. The first is the quality of our food. Too much of our food is poisoned with synthetic pesticides, fertilizers, hormones, antibiotics, and harmful bacteria. All of these substances combine in our bodies to trigger intense immune-system reactions and ongoing inflammation, both of which accelerate aging and lead to skin problems and major disease.

The second problem is that most of our food is processed, which, as discussed in chapter 2, indicates an overabundance of calories and artificial ingredients. A diet rich in processed food ultimately causes obesity and sickness. If the quality of our food is substantially improved, the result will be better nourishment, satisfaction, and beauty. If you are overweight, you will lose weight without trying.

I urge you to buy fresh, organic or biodynamic, antioxidant-rich whole grains, vegetables, and fruits, and to reduce as much as possible all processed foods as well as conventionally raised animal foods. I am not, however, going to ask you to deprive yourself of any of your favorite foods. On the contrary, if you are a lover of chocolate, for example, I recommend that you buy the highest quality, such as Repunzell chocolate, made from biodynamic ingredients. If you enjoy animal foods, I urge you to buy animal foods that have been raised organically or biodynamically.

You don't have to diet to improve your health, beauty, or weight. You just have to improve the quality of your food and then add regular gentle exercise.

Concerns About Price

People argue that cost is a factor when it comes to buying organic or biodynamic food. It's true that organic and biodynamic foods are often more expensive at the checkout counter, but if you purchase these high-quality foods, you will actually be more satisfied with your diet, have fewer cravings, eat less, and experience far greater health and beauty.

Consider a hidden cost in our food today: the cost of medical care. The more poisons you consume, the sicker you become and the greater your risk of major illness grows. The foods we eat are the primary reason we must make so many visits to the doctor and the hospital and why so many of us are dependent on pharmaceutical drugs. Those costs are enormous. The higher the quality of your food, the better your health, and the less dependent you will be on medical care, especially as you age.

Tips for Making Food Preparation Easier

To cut down on the time needed to prepare healthful and delicious meals, I recommend that you cook larger quantities on the weekend. Prepare a large pot of whole grains, another of soup, and still another of beans. These foods can be refrigerated and reheated during the week when you arrive home after a busy day.

Vegetables are health and beauty fast foods. You can boil or steam greens in less than seven minutes. Simply rinse the greens, put about an inch of water in the bottom of a pot, place the greens in a steamer, and the steamer in the pot. Cover and turn up the flame to medium-high. Steam for three to seven minutes, depending on the thickness of the greens, and you've made a high-fiber, high-antioxidant, high-phytochemical, low-calorie snack. Purchase organic sauces and dressings to enhance the flavor of your vegetables, if you like.

Make enough food every evening to have leftovers for lunch the following day. You can place the food in plastic containers and bring them to your office, or simply reheat them at home. You'll have a healthful and delicious lunch every day.

Soak grains the night before cooking them to make them more digestible and their nutrients easier to assimilate. If you prefer, you can add a teaspoon of apple cider vinegar to the soaking water to promote a fermenting process, which further aids digestion.

The recommendations that follow offer suggestions for seven days' worth of breakfast and dinner meals. Menu plans are also provided in chapter 9 for further planning. This shorter version of the menu plan will help you establish a healing diet and a natural rhythm through the week. Monday's breakfast, for example, includes the cooked whole grain quinoa; Tuesday's features oats. Monday's dinner includes cod; Tuesday's spinach salad. Many of us are at a loss when considering what to cook each night. On this program, you will know exactly what to prepare. As this rhythm becomes a habit, you will naturally make adjustments without having to think too much about what you'll be eating each day.

You may already have a good rhythm with your dinner meals. In that case, you may only want to substitute some of the ingredients to improve their quality. Of course, you can modify these suggestions any way you like. Try to make all your food choices organic or biodynamic.

Items to Purchase Before Starting the Program

Skin Care Products

I urge you to purchase or make skin care products whose ingredients are organic or biodynamically grown plant substances.

1. A facial cleanser

2. A body cleanser

3. A toner

4. A moisturizer

5. Bath and body oils

6. Essential plant oils to be used in footbaths

above Essential oils can be used in baths, footbaths, and body oils

Food Items

The following are whole, unprocessed grains and fresh vegetables and fruits to be used in your breakfast, lunch, and dinner meals. Whenever possible, grains should be organically or biodynamically grown.

1. Dried, jarred, or canned beans, preferably organic. Jarred or canned can simply be reheated. Dried beans must be reconstituted and cooked.

2. Brown rice, short-, medium-, or long-grain—whichever you prefer. Short-grain rice tends to be heartier, firmer, and nuttier in flavor; medium- and long-grain are milder and softer.

3. Seven-grain cereal.

4. A wide variety of fresh fruits.

5. Millet.

6. Miso, a fermented soybean paste, used as a base for soups, stews, and sauces. It is available in natural foods stores in plastic tubs. I recommend South River Miso, one of the highest-quality misos produced today. (See recipes.) Add 1 tablespoon miso per cup of soup stock for a wonderful, savory flavor. Miso is a powerful healing food and it is thought to be very protective against a wide array of illnesses, including cancer.

7. Oats, either as oatmeal, which cooks quickly, or as steel-cut oat groats (also known as Irish oats), which must boil for about 20 minutes in order to be fully cooked. Irish oats are crunchier. Many people find them more flavorful than instant or rolled oats.

8. Quinoa.

9. Rye.

10. Spelt

11. A variety of squashes and sweet vegetables, such as acorn, butternut, buttercup, Hokkaido pumpkin, and carrots, beets, and rutabaga.

12. A variety of green and leafy vegetables, such as bok choy, broccoli, collard greens, kale, mustard greens, napa cabbage, and watercress.

All of these items can be purchased at your local natural foods store.

left Whole grains are rich in antioxidants.

Following the Program

Nine of the twelve steps to healing beauty can be employed every day. Some are morning activities; others are intended to be done at lunch and during the afternoon, while the remaining daily activities are done at night. Step 8 suggests that you choose one day a week for a healing bath, facial mask, or footbath. Steps 11 and 12 are meant to be carried out on the weekends. Again, choose the activities that feel right for you.

A note about the morning sequence. I have suggested that your first activity be a morning meditation or affirmation. Your second is morning skin care, which includes a shower. You may reverse the order if you prefer. Do whatever suits your natural rhythm best.

Step 1. Morning Meditation and Affirmation

The day begins with a morning meditation or affirmation. Let's say that you wake up at 6 or 7 A.M. After rising, sit comfortably in a chair or on a meditation pillow and meditate for five to ten minutes. Do any form of meditation that puts you in touch with your inner feelings, rhythms, and goals for the day ahead. You can read a poem, an inspirational passage, or a section from spiritual literature. You can also choose one of the meditations provided in chapter 1. To enhance your concentration and to create a more relaxed mood, you might consider lighting a candle.

Among the meditations we at Dr. Hauschka recommend are the seven "precepts of the day." These precepts are designed to guide us in our actions throughout the day and to help us observe our inner feelings, behaviors, and rhythms as the day progresses. In effect, the precept of the day is a tool for staying present and being mindful. This alone will help you stay in touch with your inner self. It also has the uncanny ability to help you remain in touch with your feelings of strength and power.

practicing beauty

123

Here are the seven precepts. Consider meditating on the precept that corresponds with each day.

Monday: Right Word. Doing a morning meditation on the right word will help you remain mindful of your words and overall speech throughout the day. Simply spend five minutes reflecting on your commitment to speak positively today and to refrain from engaging in criticism or gossip. Many people find that after doing this meditation, their mood is much better. They feel more powerful and in control of their lives.

After meditating on the right word, your speech will be more positive. At the same time, you will notice how the words of others either elevate their life energy or depress it. After a single day of observing speech, you will see how powerful the words we use every day truly are.

Tuesday: Right Action. Every situation offers an opportunity for us to take the most creative, positive, and life-enhancing action possible. Begin the day by meditating on your commitment to take the right action in every one of your behaviors and decisions today. Listen to your inner voice whenever you face an important decision. Rather than acting from superficial impulse or from emotions, seek guidance from a deeper voice or rhythm.

Meditating on the right action also allows us to become more aware of our priorities for the day. Ask yourself at the outset of your meditation, "What is the most important thing I must accomplish today?" When the answer becomes clear, commit to performing that task, whatever it may be.

Wednesday: Right Standpoint. So much of what we do comes from someone else's needs or demands. In effect, we are acting from someone else's center of gravity. By meditating on the right standpoint, we come into a deeper awareness of our sense of self. This is our place of balance, compassion, and power. Try to maintain this awareness throughout the day. Notice when you are being rushed or stressed. Notice how your balance may be upset by certain situations or certain people. When you find yourself going out of balance, spend a few minutes quietly returning to your inner rhythms and center. Once you've done that, your actions will be more effective and under control.

Thursday: Right Endeavor. Your life has a purpose and a dream. In essence, you are attempting to become the person you long to be. You do that by expressing your talents and abilities, by holding to your ideals, and by committing to excellence in all that you do. In the process, your talents and abilities emerge. With each day, you indeed become more the person you always wanted to be. Right endeavor is acting from this deep purpose you have for yourself. It is acting in harmony with your life goals and dreams.

This morning, begin the day by meditating on how you can make a step in your life's progress. What can you do today that will be a greater expression of who you are and what you are capable of doing and achieving? As the day unfolds, notice how you are being given opportunities to express those abilities.

Friday: Right Memory. Memory can be a source of joy, pain, and learning. Start the day by meditating on a few of your many accomplishments. Remember how you overcame obstacles and succeeded in the face of challenges. Realize that your memory can be a source of learning and evolution. Throughout the day, be alert to how previous experiences, both good and bad, have helped you succeed and fulfill your dreams.

Saturday: Right Opinion. Begin the day by meditating on the extent to which you create negative dialogues inside your head. Consider that opinions can make all of us stubborn and negative. They create inflexibility and conflict—usually needless—in our relationships. As you progress through the day, observe the extent to which opinions are preventing you from being open and objective with others. Also observe how opinions insert themselves in your interactions to create unnecessary conflict.

As an antidote to opinion, practice truly listening to each person who speaks to you today—that is, listening to the other person while maintaining an empty mind. Do not think about what you will say in response; rather, take in all that the person is saying and then wait for your inner rhythm to inform you of what needs to be said. As much as possible, brush aside negative opinions and judgments of others.

Sunday: Right Resolve. Commit to love. Love is an action. Love yourself in practical ways, such as following this program as much as possible. Begin the day by meditating on how grateful you are for your life and your beauty. Commit to showing your love to your family or friends. Let people know how grateful you are for their presence in your life.

By doing these meditations for just five or ten minutes each day, you will find that you can easily attune yourself to your inner rhythms. You will notice that your sense of self—the center of your being—is stronger. This is the basis for greater self-love. Think of the above mental exercises as a yoga for your inner life. These exercises will make you more conscious of your thoughts, feelings, and actions, which will lead you to a new freedom.

Step 2. Morning Skin Care

If you are using the basic approach to morning skin care, you will need a facial cleanser, a body cleanser, a body oil, a toner, and a moisturizer (see pages 70–83). I also encourage you to try aromatherapy in your shower or bath. The essential oils of rosemary and lemon are wonderful morning oils. They stimulate circulation and energize the body. If you are attempting to heal a specific skin condition, such as acne or rosacea, I urge you to adopt one of the healing regimens described in chapter 5.

Cleansing

We cleanse the skin in the morning in order to wash away impurities that were excreted from the skin during sleep. Place a small amount of cleanser—about $1/2$ inch—in the palm of your moist hand and rinse your face and neck thoroughly, either under the shower or in a basin of warm water.

A good facial cleanser contains almond puree mixed with extracts of organic herbs such as anthyllis, calendula, and rose. The facial cleanser should exfoliate gently, leaving new cells intact.

In Your Shower

Use a natural organic body wash that cleanses the body but doesn't strip it of its natural moisture. You can also put a few drops of rosemary concentrate on a loofah and gently rub your body, paying particular attention to the places where lymph nodes are concentrated, such as the armpits and groin and behind the knees. The rosemary enhances circulation in these areas.

Body Oils

Protect your body skin for the day ahead by applying a high-quality body oil or body moisturizer, rich in plant essential oil, which will balance your skin and keep it warm and moist throughout the day. The finer body moisturizers contain essential oils from any of the following medicinal plants: lavender, rosemary, lemon, spruce, blackthorn, and arnica. Lavender, which calms, strengthens, and supports the nervous system, is recommended when you are under stress.

Toner

After drying your body, gently blot your face dry with a cotton towel and then apply a gentle toner, one made from organic or biodynamic extracts and essences. A good toner will prepare the skin for a daily moisturizer.

Moisturizer

Moisturizers should protect the skin but also encourage the skin's own moisturizing functions. Use a moisturizer made from the highest-quality healing plants. Among the ingredients you'll want in your moisturizer are essential oils of anthyllis, witch hazel, Saint-John's-wort, and calendula, and wheat germ, olive, and jojoba oils. A good moisturizer will balance dry, mature, and normal skin.

Moisturizers can be changed based on the seasons, as the weather makes different demands on your skin. In severe winter climates, you will need more protection. Good winter moisturizers often contain healing plants, such as marshmallow, avocado, Saint-John's-wort, rose petal, and rose hip. These protect the epidermis and soothe and heal skin irritated by harsh weather.

For spring and summer, a good moisturizer is one containing an array of healing herbs such as quince seed, marshmallow, and witch hazel. These soothe and heal but do not provide the same level of heavy protection that a winter moisturizer does.

Eye Care

Apply a fine eye cream made with castor oil, beeswax, and rosewax. Use it sparingly to protect the delicate tissue around the eyes. Use your eye cream in the morning, not at night, so your skin can breathe and heal while you sleep.

How Does Your Morning Care Feel?

Once you have cleansed, toned, and moisturized your face, feel your skin. It should feel relaxed, yet bright and alive. It should not be tight or in any way uncomfortable. Your skin care regimen should, in essence, be a healing program that results in even more beautiful skin. If your face feels tight or oily, or if blemishes arise, your skin is likely in rebellion against a product, or products, that contain synthetic ingredients. For the most beautiful skin, use products made of healing plants that were grown organically or biodynamically.

Step 3. Healing Breakfast

This seven-day menu plan, along with the menus and recipes in chapter 9, will help you establish a morning and evening meal rhythm that is easy to follow and maintain. I recommend that you simply repeat this menu four times, plus two days, for the full thirty-day program.

The morning meal comprises cooked whole grains. Each kind of grain has a distinctive, subtle flavor. All provide an array of essential and healing benefits, including vitamin E, protein, other vitamins, minerals, and fiber. Whole grains are energy foods. They are rich in complex carbohydrates, which are slowly absorbed and provide long-lasting energy throughout the day. They also promote healthy digestion. You will recall from chapter 3 that digestion is a key to healthy and beautiful skin. Cooked whole grains are a key to good digestion and elimination.

All of these grains require twenty-five minutes or less of cooking time. Remember that you have been soaking the morning grain from the previous night. Develop the habit of starting to soak the following day's grains while preparing today's breakfast. (For cooking instructions and ways to enhance the flavor of your breakfast grains, see chapter 9, "Menus and Recipes for Healthy and Beautiful Skin.")

Here is the morning menu:

Monday: Quinoa. Quinoa is regarded by nutritionists as a superfood for its protein, vitamin, and mineral content.

Tuesday: Oat Groats. Oat groats are a whole grain packed with nutrients. Prepared like a hot cereal, they have a warm, nutty flavor.

Wednesday: Seven-Grain Cereal. Seven-grain cereal is available in bulk at most natural foods stores. It provides a wide variety of grains, is rich in flavor, and is especially hearty in winter.

Thursday: Millet. Millet is a high-protein grain that's rich in nutrients and has a mild, delicious flavor.

Friday: Spelt. A high-protein grain, spelt is rich in flavor.

Saturday. Poached eggs on sprouted grain toast with smoked salmon (optional).

Sunday. Buckwheat pancakes topped with organic yogurt and maple syrup served with one or two organic breakfast sausage links or bacon, if desired.

Step 4. Healing Lunch

Your lunch will consist of leftovers from the previous night's dinner. When you leave the house, be sure to bring the following:

- A piece of fruit to be eaten as a snack later in the day.

- A bottle of water.

- A thermos containing vegetable soup or herbal tea.

The first thing to do at lunchtime is to unwind. Go off by yourself for a few minutes, if you can. Relax, breathe, and feel your body release its tension. Drink your soup; eat your lunch. Really taste it. If you eat consciously and chew your food thoroughly, you will enjoy your meal and feel more satisfied when you're done. You'll also be less tempted to snack between meals. This approach will do wonders for your digestion, too. If time and weather permit, take a short stroll after you eat to get fresh air, further release tension, and restore your energy.

Step 5. Afternoon Walk

Take a five- or ten-minute walk at lunch every day. Don't worry about your distance or speed. Remember, you are walking according to your own rhythms. If you're feeling energized, walk faster; if you want to relax, stroll.

Even a short walk relieves tension and stress. It elevates the heart rate, improves circulation, and stretches muscles to provide greater range of motion. It can also strengthen your bones. Researchers have found that three ten-minute walks per day have the same effect on your fitness as a single thirty-minute walk—and thirty minutes of walking per day significantly improves weight, muscle tone, and cardiovascular fitness.

I have found that physical activity—even short walks—increases my energy, enhances my ability to concentrate, and strengthens my will. The short walk is an underappreciated activity; it provides many more benefits than most people realize.

Step 6. Healing Dinner

The emphasis here is on quality, simplicity, and a rich assortment of vegetables. Be sure that your animal foods, such as poultry, red meat, or wild fish, are raised organically or biodynamically. The seven-day menu provided is a series of suggestions to help you decide what to eat at night. Make any substitutions you like. I do urge you to sustain a rhythm in your menu planning. I always like to think of Tuesdays, for example, as fish night, and Wednesdays as pasta and/or vegetarian. This approach makes planning and shopping much easier, and the children like knowing what to expect. As long as the meals are delicious, the routine can be easy to maintain. (See chapter 9, "Menus and Recipes for Healthy and Beautiful Skin," for healing dinner recipes.)

Healing Dinner Menus

Monday

Cod with Sautéed Vegetables (page 132)

steamed swiss chard

Wild Rice Salad (page 163)

Tuesday

Vegetable and Bean–Stuffed Squash (page 179)

spinach salad topped with feta

Wednesday

Pepper Quiche (page 195)

steamed kale

Simple Grated Carrot Salad (page 170)

Thursday

Chicken with a Miso-Honey Glaze (page 189)

Quick and Easy Oven-Grilled Asparagus (page 168)

Skillet-Roasted Lima Beans with Herbs (page 178)

Friday

Whole-Wheat Linguine with Broccoli (page 162)

Vegetables with Mustard Vinaigrette (page 171)

Fresh Figs and Honey (page 198)

Saturday

Beef Stew (page 188)

steamed green beans

rustic bread

Sunday

Mixed-Pea Soup (page 154)

steamed cauliflower

Frozen Berry-Banana Parfait (page 198)

Step 7. Healing Evening Care

When you are ready in the evenings, use your organic facial cleanser to remove makeup and wash your face. What's important about this step is the quality of the product you use and the way in which you touch your skin. If the product is composed of synthetic ingredients, chances are that it's harming to your skin and accelerating the aging process. On the other hand, if you do this step with a high-quality cleanser and treat your skin with loving-kindness, you are actually healing your skin, relieving yourself of tension, and enhancing your beauty. Always follow the cleansing with either a water-based toner or a conditioner. Remember, no night creams.

Step 8. Healing Bath and Facial Mask

Choose a particular night of each week, say Thursday, to pamper yourself, relax, and beautify your skin by taking one of the following healing baths or a footbath and applying a facial mask. Try to do this ritual rhythmically, meaning at the same time and on the same day each week. This will make the bath and facial much more therapeutic.

You can do the same bath and facial over and over again. You can also choose a bath that will balance your current temperament, as described in chapter 1. Remember the four temperaments and their related baths.

- Cholerics take a lavender bath to relax and relieve tension.

- Sanguines take a spruce bath to ground and focus.

- Phlegmatics take a lemon bath to break up stagnation, awaken the nervous system, and warm the body.

- Melancholics take a rosemary bath to warm the body, boost the circulation, elevate the mood, and ignite the inner fire.

Remember that when you draw your bath, potentize the water by creating a figure-8 vortex. As you do that, think beautiful thoughts.

A Special Rejuvenating Nutritive Bath

If you are exhausted, it shows. Your beauty is dulled and cannot shine forth. At Dr. Hauschka, we recommend a special rejuvenating bath whenever we have given way too much and are burned out. Here's the formula.

Run a warm bath that would be an appropriate temperature for a baby. Add 1 cup of the best-quality (unpasteurized, organic if possible) milk available, along with 1 egg (again, organic). Place 1 whole lemon under the water and slice the peel with a knife in several places to release its oils. Squeeze the lemon into the tub to release its juices. With large, slow movements, circulate the water gently in a figure 8 to potentize and enliven it.

Continue to circulate the water for a few minutes until you feel the water is soft. Leave the lemon in the water and enter the tub. Stay for 7 to 10 minutes only. This should be a peaceful, quiet time. Dry off without rinsing. Pat dry gently rather than rubbing. The silky quality of the bathwater leaves the skin soft to the touch without being sticky. Go to bed immediately, being sure to feel snug and warm, and rest for at least 20 minutes.

This bath has enormous powers to restore and rejuvenate. It can be repeated daily for three to seven days, and then once or twice a week until you feel fully recovered.

Special Footbath

We can eliminate a great deal of stress and toxic emotion simply by caring for our feet.

On nights when you cannot take a full bath, try soaking your feet in an enamel bowl or a plastic tub filled with very warm water and a bath concentrate. If you are staying home that night, use essential oils of spruce, lavender, or sage, all of which relax and draw toxins and stagnant emotions from your tissues. If you are going out, use rosemary or lemon, which will leave your feet feeling like they are dancing on air.

Soak your feet for at least 10 minutes. Dry them off and brush them with a loofah or a natural-bristle body brush.

Gently massage into the tissues of your feet and nails a strengthening and healing essential oil such as neem, apricot kernel oil, lavender, or chamomile. Apply a moisturizer when you are finished.

As you give your feet all this love, get in touch with them. They take a pounding every day. Find the tender spots and gently massage them. If your feet are dry and cracked, apply a foot cream with healing herbs such as rosemary or goldenseal, rice starch, and silk to restore circulation and a healthy environment for the skin tissue.

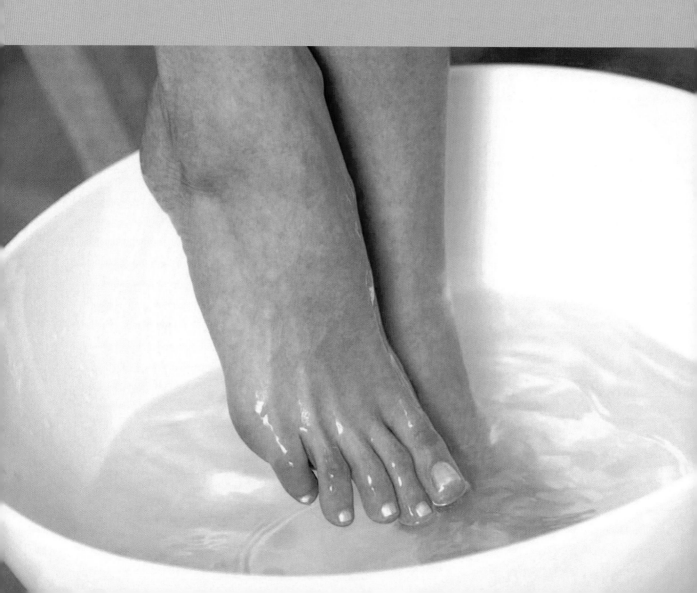

Detox Footbaths

This is a special footbath designed to remove physical and emotional toxins.

Soak your feet in a bowl of very warm water with 1 tablespoon ground mustard and 1 teaspoon cayenne pepper for 10 to 15 minutes. Add very warm water to the footbath occasionally to maintain the temperature. Once you are done, dry your feet and drink 8 ounces warm water with the juice of 1 lemon in it. The lemon drink is a traditional tonic for the liver. It also helps overcome constipation.

Healing Facial Masks

You can choose from a wide variety of wonderful facial masks. For example, you could do an intensive facial cleansing by applying a healing clay mask. Or you could alternate masks—on one night do a cleansing mask, on another a rejuvenating mask, and on still another a moisturizing mask. See chapter 4 for an array of generic masks that contain healing herbal plants.

In addition, Dr. Hauschka offers several healing masks, including the following:

- Facial Steam Bath
- Cleansing Clay Mask
- Rejuvenating Mask
- Moisturizing Mask
- Firming Mask, which is especially recommended for women age fifty and above.

Step 9. Record Your Thoughts

While you are relaxing in your bath or wearing your mask, many thoughts, emotions, and insights will come to mind. This is a great time to record your thoughts in a journal. Journaling gets you back in touch with your rhythms, cleanses the soul, and restores inner equilibrium. Write for ten, twenty, or thirty minutes. Explore your feelings, purge yourself of what burdens you, or celebrate your achievements.

Step 10. Healing Night Care

As stated in chapter 4, refrain from applying moisturizer at night, as the skin attempts to eliminate waste through the pores at night, and any substance that coats the skin only makes the job harder. Night moisturizing also encourages the blocking of pores and leads to various disorders, including blemishes.

If you are reluctant to give up night creams, I recommend that you gradually wean yourself of them over the course of this thirty-day period. During the first week, use about a quarter less moisturizer than you normally use. Reduce that by a quarter more each week until you are finally free of the night creams entirely.

Simply cleanse and tone your face thoroughly and allow it to breathe and eliminate through the night. If you would like to use some kind of nighttime skin care product, I recommend the Dr. Hauschka Rhythmic Night Conditioner.

An Evening of Looking Back

Complete the day by doing Rudolf Steiner's meditation in which you look back on your day's events in reverse—that is, think first about whatever occurred in the evening and then reflect on the day as if you were moving backward through time. This powerful meditation will yield new insights into yourself, your circumstances, and the people around you.

Step 11. A Healing Weekend

As much as possible, let your weekend be a time of rest and recovery. The more television you watch, the more time you spend on the computer, the less relaxed your body is. Set time aside each weekend to unplug from technology—the telephone, the television, the Palm Pilot, and the computer. This is yet another way of recovering your sense of self and your natural rhythms. Think of this time as a time to heal and fast from technology.

I recommend four activities that will enhance your weekend and stimulate healing. Choose any one of the four, combination of the four, or all four activities. Each has the potential to make a healing difference in your life.

1. Do Nothing

If possible, set aside at least twenty minutes every weekend to do nothing. Just feel your feelings, experience your rhythms, and feel the beautiful rest that comes over you when you have nothing at all to do.

2. Get a Massage

If you can, get a massage on the weekend. Many massage schools offer reduced rates on weekends so that their students can practice and learn their craft. Call your local massage school and find out what it is offering.

If you can, get at least two massages every month. Try to schedule your massage on the same day of the week, and roughly the same time of the day, in order to establish a rhythm that will reinforce its healing effects.

3. Take a Long Walk

Take time for a long walk every weekend, if possible. As discussed in chapter 1, you need not power walk. Instead, start out at a comfortable pace, and as you progress, increase or decrease your speed depending on how your body is reacting. Speed is not as important as distance and time. Increase the distance and time you walk as your fitness improves—and if you walk regularly, your fitness *will* improve. Whenever possible, walk in nature—a forest, a beach, or a park. Most important of all, enjoy your walk.

As you are walking, notice nature. See its beauty. Feel how it is feeding you with love and gratitude. Find something on your path that strikes you as beautiful and bring it home. It's a gift from nature. Display it in a special place and notice it again and again throughout the week.

Each season, I create a nature table on which I place plants, crystals, a beautiful card, flowers, and art I've discovered on my walks. Recently, I got my florist to supply a few organic and biodynamic flowers, which I now purchase regularly. Many farmers' markets also sell organic flowers. All of these gifts from nature are an inspiration to me. I want them displayed prominently in my home because they remind me of the love that is constantly flowing from nature.

4. Care for Your Hair

A wonderful treatment for hair that's been damaged by chemical treatments, sun, wind, chlorine, or heat is to apply a hair lotion made of healing herbs, followed by healing essential oils. Here's how you can do it.

Apply a hair lotion that contains herbal extracts to your hair for five to ten minutes, massaging your scalp thoroughly. The extracts should include some of the following: neem, nettle, calendula, rosemary, and arnica. Begin exploring your scalp gently with

your fingertips in gentle, circular motions. You may find tender spots, especially at the base of the skull. Give these areas a little extra attention and loving care. Move the scalp until it's loose and relaxed. Then brush your hair with a natural-bristle hairbrush for several minutes. Bend forward at the waist and brush from the base of the skull forward. Run the brush gently through the hair. This further massages the scalp and distributes the oil to the hair strands. Brush slowly, gently, and firmly.

Apply about 1 tablespoon of a hair oil made of extracts such as neem, wheat germ oil, chamomile, and rosemary. Run it through the hair, beginning at the scalp but concentrating on the ends. Comb the oil through with your fingers or a large-tooth comb. Cover your hair with a woolen hat or a cotton scarf and leave it on for at least an hour. If you want to protect the hat or the scarf from stains, put on a loose-fitting shower cap first. This will work up a little heat and help the oil penetrate more into the hair. The treatment may be left on overnight.

Shampoo thoroughly that night or the next morning. You may need an extra application of shampoo to remove excess oil. Rinse with diluted apple cider vinegar (2 quarts water to 2 tablespoons vinegar) before applying conditioner.

Step 12. Healing the Past, Embracing the Future: Write Your Biography

Special Project: Your Biography and Life Cycles

One of the principle benefits of this thirty-day period of Practicing Beauty is self-discovery, which is part of healing your inner beauty. Insights will arise naturally—as you prepare your meals, write in your journal, and walk in the park. But there is a powerful exercise you can do to obtain new and additional insights into your life. That exercise is to organize your life in seven-year periods and record the major events that occurred in each. Do this exercise over the entire month, adding new bits of information as they emerge. At the conclusion of the month, you will feel you know yourself better. Very likely, you'll also have a much clearer picture of where you are going and what you want to become.

Go through each year of your life and note important family events, such as celebrations, birthdays, vacations, trips, illnesses, deaths, and moves, or family lore. To stimulate your memory, ask a family member what he or she remembers about you.

Begin with the ages of birth to seven. Try to record at least five important events or trends that occurred during your childhood. Perhaps you have a particularly strong memory of your mother, or father, or of going to school. Perhaps you associate several important events with your first couple of years at school.

Do the same for each seven-year period of your life. When you are done, record the events as headlines on a U-shaped chart. The first thirty-two or thirty-three years or so form the downward part of the chart. This is the period in which you are grounding into your body, your nature, and your connection to the earth. After age

practicing beauty

137

thirty-three, you start to ascend the U-chart. This is the spiritualizing period, the time in which many previously dormant yet important gifts and abilities start to emerge.

Look at the chart for patterns, clues, and new insights into yourself. Consider that you're researching a heroic figure in a story or a fairy tale. What do you see about yourself? What ambition or dream are you attempting to manifest?

If you work at this over the entire thirty-day period, you may be surprised at how much you remember and what surprising insights emerge. The purpose is not to dwell on the past or to engage in painful memories but rather to develop a relationship with yourself based on love, compassion, and deeper understanding.

I was amazed to see my own biography. I had thought of myself as strong and healthy, but I was quite sickly as a child. I also noticed that in my youth I was highly impressionable and strongly attracted to dynamic, charismatic men. As I began my path of healing beauty, I gradually became a more dynamic person myself. My creativity and leadership abilities started to emerge. I also became more self-nurturing. As I did, I attracted my husband, Clifford, who is a strong yet nurturing man himself. Do this exercise. You will be amazed at what you learn about yourself.

A Time for You

Taken together, these twelve steps may seem like a lot. As I said, not all of them must be done collectively. Most, however, can be incorporated into your life—and the more you do, the greater the reward. Remember, this lunar period is a time for you to heal, enhance your beauty, and reconnect with your inner self. All of us need time and energy; these are fundamental to life itself. Unless you take the time to care for yourself, you will not have the energy to live the life you want. Your beauty will grow more radiant as you love and care for yourself. And then all seven of the blessings I listed earlier will be yours.

Celebrate the Month

At the conclusion of your thirty-day program, take stock. Notice the changes that have occurred with your skin, your feelings about yourself, your outlook on life, and your relationships at home and at work. See how smooth and shining your skin has become. Recognize that some burden has been lifted from you and how that change has affected your appearance. Reread what you wrote in your journal during the past month and notice any changes that have occurred in your inner and outer life. See how a month of self-love can heal your beauty.

Whenever I complete a particular course or achieve a goal I set for myself, I like to celebrate. I often buy myself a small gift or a bouquet of roses. Give yourself a gift at the conclusion of your monthlong program. Consider ultimately making some version of these twelve steps to healing beauty a way of life.

Chapter 8

Sustainable Beauty:
How Beauty Affects Our World

Beauty is among the most personal of subjects. To a great extent, our beauty determines the success or failure of our lives. Consequently, when we think about beauty, we tend to think about our own beauty. When we purchase a particular beauty product, we think about its impact on our own beauty.

There is also a deeper truth that we don't often consider, but that affects us nonetheless. Your beauty, and all that you do to make yourself more beautiful, can change the world. The skin care products you use, the food you eat, and the clothing you wear—just to name a few of your beauty-related choices—can have a rippling effect: on one hand, they give you many personal rewards, but on the other, they affect the entire planet, giving greater beauty and happiness to all. This is part of the remarkable and mysterious nature of beauty. Ultimately, it is linked to everything we do. It helps shape our world.

True beauty—that is, beauty that arises from a loving heart and youthful, radiant skin—is based on health. The more you use substances that injure your skin or adversely affect the health of your body, the more you will be forced to hide yourself behind elaborate clothing, makeup, or extreme makeovers, all of which are illusions of beauty.

True beauty arises when you rely primarily on skin care products and foods whose ingredients were grown organically or biodynamically. These foods and products can restore the beauty of your skin, give you more energy, protect you from illness, promote optimal weight, and create within you a deep sense of well-being. These are reasons enough to eat healing foods and utilize high-quality products. And they seem like rather small steps—so small, in fact, that virtually every one of us can do them. Remarkably, the foods and skin care products that have the most enhancing effect on our beauty also help heal the environment and sustain the earth.

We have only just begun to think about sustainability, which is the capacity to meet our society's current needs while providing for the needs of future generations. Right now, most of the ways we grow food, conduct business, and run our economy are unsustainable, meaning they are robbing future generations of the resources they will need to survive and thrive. We can, however, work to change this behavior and restore our world.

One of the simplest places to start is to understand the vast difference between fertilizer and fertility. Fertilizers are chemicals used to support one generation of plants. These chemicals allow us to produce food today, but they weaken our ability to produce food in the future.

Fertility, on the other hand, is a condition that allows plants, animals, and humans to reproduce. Fertility meets our immediate needs—it creates nutritious, hardy, and healthy plants—and, at the same time, provides for future generations.

Biodynamic and organic farmers use natural and organic compost and crop rotation to restore the earth's humus content and support its fertility. The earth grows stronger and healthier as these methods are employed. This is sustainable agriculture. These methods not only meet our needs but our children's needs, and their children's needs.

When you choose organic and biodynamic foods and skin care products, you are shifting dollars away from nonsustainable methods to the type of farming that might be called *healing agriculture*. In the process, you are demanding that American industry and the worldwide economy base their practices on what is good for each of us today as well as those who will inherit the earth tomorrow.

This is the spirit of Dr. Hauschka Skin Care. Rudolf Hauschka had a dream: to create pharmaceutical remedies that healed both humanity and the earth. He set out to produce the most effective and highest-quality natural remedies—medicines that not only addressed illness but also, more important, promoted health. Hauschka wanted his medicines, unlike the pharmaceutical drugs prescribed today, to have no side effects.

We need to support our local organic and biodynamic farmers. Community-based farms that use sustainable methods are springing up throughout the United States. Local people buy shares in the farm and make weekly or twice weekly visits to pick up produce. The result: The farmers have a guaranteed income, and local people have a guaranteed source of healthy food. Both sides benefit. We should all support our local farmers, especially those who use sustainable methods, by shopping in farmer's markets and at local farm stands.

If we are to restore our health and beauty and heal the earth, we must become conscious of our dependence on the health of the soil and the labor of those who act as its stewards. Part of that awareness is to be willing to pay a little more for organic and biodynamic foods and skin care products. The rewards from this investment are greater beauty, health, and economic stability, and a greener earth—the basis for peace among us all.

Chapter 9

Menus and Recipes
for Healthy and Beautiful Skin

This chapter contains a suggested menu for a week, and sixty recipes. You may follow my plan, or substitute any recipe from the choices offered with one of your favorite recipes. Finding a rhythm for your meals is essential to your beauty and health. Remember, we are beings of rhythm, and rhythm supports and carries life. Try to establish a rhythm to your meals. For instance, if you usually eat breakfast at 7 A.M., stick to that time as often as possible.

Another way to establish rhythm is to choose specific days for particular meals. For example, have quinoa for breakfast on Mondays. You can vary what you choose to top your quinoa with, but plan to have quinoa each Monday. Monday dinner can always be fish. You will begin to find that you become more creative, as well as more efficient with your time, once you have a structure for the week. The Dr. Hauschka Way to Awakening Beauty is about becoming conscious of your daily choices. You will find that rhythm carries and enlivens your choices. Please use biodynamic or organic ingredients as much as possible. Introduce what you can into your life and slowly you will transform how you view and eat food. Food becomes an artistic expression of who you are rather than a burden. Remember, quality over quantity. I recommend that during this "twelve steps to Awakening Beauty" month you ease into your transition by using frozen or canned beans, as well as roasted red peppers and artichokes from a can or a jar. As you feel more comfortable with the new recipes, you may institute changes such as preparing beans from scratch, roasting your own peppers, cooking artichokes, and so on.

7-Day Menu

	Breakfast	Lunch*	Dinner
Monday	quinoa with chopped pecans cooked in an orange juice—water mixture topped with milk, rice milk, oat milk, yogurt, or crème fraîche	salad with hard-boiled eggs, roasted red peppers, olives, smoked trout, and tomatoes	Cod with Sautéed Vegetables (page 182) steamed Swiss chard Wild Rice Salad (page 163)
Tuesday	steel-cut oat groats** with apples and almonds	Wild Rice Salad (page 163) salad greens	Vegetable and Bean-Stuffed Squash (page 179) spinach salad topped with feta
Wednesday	seven-grain cereal with raisins	Vegetable and Bean-Stuffed Squash (page 179) on a bed of lettuce	Pepper Quiche (page 195) steamed kale Simple Grated Carrot Salad (page 170)
Thursday	millet with apricots	Pepper Quiche (page 195) kale and carrots	Chicken with a Miso-Honey Glaze (page 189) Quick and Easy Oven-Grilled Asparagus (page 168) Skillet-Roasted Lima Beans with Herbs (page 178)
Friday	spelt with chopped dates	chicken with roasted lima beans on a bed of mesclun or lettuce	Whole-Wheat Linguine with Broccoli (page 162) Vegetables with Mustard Vinaigrette (page 171) Fresh Figs and Honey† (page 198)
Saturday	poached, soft-boiled, or scrambled eggs with sprouted-grain toast, smoked salmon, and butter (optional)	Whole-Wheat Linguine with Broccoli (page 162) vegetables	Beef Stew (page 188) steamed green beans rustic bread
Sunday	buckwheat pancakes	Beef Stew (page 188)	Mixed-Pea Soup (page 154) steamed cauliflower Frozen Berry-Banana Parfait (page 198)

*Feel free to substitute leftovers from the previous evening's meal for any suggested lunch menu.
**All grains are cooked in water (with the exception of quinoa, as noted).
†Desserts are optional; I offer two per week. Several recipes are easily doubled and can be used throughout the week.

Soups

Bean and Roasted Root Vegetable Soup

Butternut Squash Bisque

Curried Broccoli Soup

Greek Olive Soup with Beans and Rice

Green Soup

Lentil–Mushroom Stew

Lentil-Spinach Soup

Mixed–Pea Soup

Potato Leek–Miso Soup

Bean and Roasted Root Vegetable Soup

Serves 6 to 8

1 leek, trimmed and cut into
   $1/2$-inch slices
3 cups root vegetables, such as
   carrots, potatoes, turnips,
   rutabaga, burdock, daikon,
   celery root, parsnips, and fennel,
   cut into $1/2$-inch slices
10 garlic cloves
1 tablespoon butter, melted
Salt and freshly ground black
   pepper
$1/2$ cup cooked beans, such as
   adzuki, kidney, or navy
4 cups vegetable broth or miso
   broth
1 teaspoon grated fresh ginger
1 tablespoon rice wine vinegar
Tamari

Preheat the oven to 350°F.

Place the leek, root vegetables, and garlic in a roasting pan and toss with the melted butter. Season with salt and pepper to taste. Roast the vegetables for 25 to 30 minutes, or until they are a deep golden brown. Add the beans, broth, grated ginger, and vinegar. Bring to a boil and simmer for 10 minutes. Season with tamari.

Butternut Squash Bisque

Serves 6 to 8

1 tablespoon butter
2 to 3 pounds butternut squash,
   peeled and diced into 1-inch
   cubes
3 large carrots, chopped
1 medium onion, chopped
1 tablespoon minced fresh ginger
2 quarts water, chicken broth, or
   vegetable broth
2 tablespoons grated orange zest
1 bunch parsley, leaves only,
   chopped
Pinch of ground nutmeg
Salt and white pepper

In a large pot, heat the butter over medium heat. Sauté the squash, carrots, onion, and ginger for 3 minutes, until they are lightly browned. Add the water and orange zest and bring to a boil. Lower the heat to a simmer and cook, uncovered, for 35 to 40 minutes, until the vegetables are tender. Add the parsley, nutmeg, and salt and pepper to taste. Puree the soup in a food processor or a blender until smooth. Return the soup to the pot and heat through.

Curried Broccoli Soup

Serves 2 to 4

1 head of broccoli, chopped
1 large onion, chopped
2 potatoes, diced
2 teaspoons curry powder
5 cups light miso broth
1 cup half-and-half
1 dash of hot pepper sauce

In a large pot, combine the broccoli, onion, potatoes, curry powder, and miso broth and simmer over medium heat for 20 minutes. Puree the mixture in batches in a food processor or a blender and pour back in the pot. Add the half-and-half and hot pepper sauce and heat through.

Greek Olive Soup with Beans and Rice

Serves 4

2 bell peppers (1 red and 1 yellow, if possible), roasted, peeled, seeded, and sliced
1 tablespoon red wine vinegar
4 tablespoons extra-virgin olive oil
Salt and freshly ground black pepper
1 leek, trimmed and chopped
1 carrot, thinly sliced
1 celery stalk, diced
2 cups steamed wild rice (millet, quinoa, or barley can be substituted)
1 cup cooked white beans
6 cups miso broth or chicken broth
2 tablespoons minced fresh oregano
2 tablespoons minced fresh savory, thyme, or rosemary
12 Kalamata olives, pitted

In a large bowl, combine the peppers with the vinegar, 2 tablespoons of the oil, and salt and pepper to taste. Cover and refrigerate for 8 hours. Heat the remaining 2 tablespoons oil in a saucepan over medium heat. Add the leek, carrot, and celery and sauté until soft, about 5 minutes. Add the rice, beans, miso, oregano, and 1 tablespoon of the savory and bring to a boil. Lower the heat and simmer, covered, for 15 minutes. Drain the peppers and add them to the soup. Stir in the olives. Taste and adjust the seasonings. Garnish with the remaining savory.

Green Soup

Serves 4 to 6

3 tablespoons butter
2 to 3 cups of a combination of finely chopped sorrel, spinach, dandelion greens, kale, Swiss chard, or any green leafy vegetable
$1/4$ cup celery, sliced thinly on the diagonal
$1/2$ cup minced green onions (green and white parts)
$1/4$ cup minced leeks
$1/4$ cup minced parsley
$1/4$ cup minced watercress
1 tablespoon flour
4 cups chicken broth or miso broth
1 cup sour cream
1 tablespoon fresh lemon juice
$1/2$ teaspoon salt
$1/4$ teaspoon freshly ground black pepper
Paprika
Croutons

In a large saucepan, heat the butter over medium heat. Add the vegetables, parsley, and watercress and sauté until wilted, about 5 minutes. Sprinkle with the flour and cook, stirring for 3 minutes. Gradually add the broth. Cook, stirring until smooth. Bring to a boil, cover, and simmer until the celery is tender, about 5 minutes. Remove from the heat. Mix $1/2$ cup hot soup with the sour cream to temper it, and then beat the sour cream mixture into the soup. Add the lemon juice, salt, and pepper. Sprinkle with paprika and serve with croutons.

Lentil-Mushroom Stew

Serves 4 to 6

3 tablespoons olive oil
1½ cups chopped onions
3 garlic cloves, finely minced
1 cup chopped carrots
1 cup chopped celery
3 cups chopped white button mushrooms
1½ cups chopped portobello mushroom caps
1 cup chopped shiitake mushroom caps
2 tablespoons tomato paste
1½ tablespoons cider vinegar
2 teaspoons paprika
1½ teaspoons cumin
2 teaspoons fennel seeds
2 cups green or brown lentils
1½ cups vegetable stock
2 cups diced canned tomatoes
2 teaspoons salt
1 teaspoon freshly ground black pepper
¼ teaspoon cayenne pepper
1 cup sliced bell pepper
1 pound fresh spinach, stemmed
1 tablespoon lemon zest

In a large sauté pan, heat the oil over medium heat. Add the onions and cook until they show a little color, about 5 minutes. Add the garlic, carrots, and celery and cook until tender, about 5 minutes. Add all the mushrooms, the tomato paste, vinegar, paprika, cumin, and fennel seeds and cook for 10 to 15 minutes. Add the lentils, stock, tomatoes, salt, pepper, and cayenne. Simmer, covered, until the lentils are tender and most of the liquid is absorbed, 20 to 25 minutes. During the last 5 minutes of simmering, add the bell pepper. Add the spinach and cook until it's wilted, about 1 minute. Stir in the lemon zest. A sauce will form around the lentils. If the lentils are too dry, add a little more stock.

Lentil-Spinach Soup

Serves 4 to 6

1 cup green or brown lentils
1 bay leaf
1 celery stalk, roughly cut
7 cups water
3 medium tomatoes, chopped, fresh or
  canned, juice reserved
1 teaspoon salt, plus additional to taste
3 tablespoons olive oil
1 large red onion, finely diced
2 garlic cloves, minced
3 tablespoons chopped parsley
7 tablespoons mellow barley miso
1 pound spinach, stemmed and cut into
  strips
Red wine vinegar
Freshly ground black pepper
Asiago, Parmesan, or Romano cheese, grated

In a soup pot, combine the lentils, bay leaf, and celery with the water, the reserved juice from the tomatoes, and ½ teaspoon salt. Bring to a slow boil. While the lentils are cooking, heat the oil in a skillet and add the onion and remaining ½ teaspoon salt; cook briskly for a few minutes, then lower the heat and stir in the garlic and parsley. Cook until the onion is soft. Add the tomatoes and combine with the lentils.

Remove ½ cup of the liquid, dissolve the miso in it, and return the liquid to the pot. When the lentils are soft, add the spinach. Once the spinach has cooked down you may need to add more water. Adjust the seasonings with vinegar, salt, and pepper. Top with grated cheese.

Mixed-Pea Soup

Serves 4 to 6

$1/4$ cup yellow split peas
$1/4$ cup green split peas
$1/2$ cup green lentils
$1/4$ cup red lentils
$4^1/2$ cups water
3 tomatoes, cored, seeded, and
  pureed
3 carrots, diced
3 garlic cloves, minced
2 chiles, diced
Juice of 1 lemon
1 teaspoon dried basil
1 teaspoon salt
$1/2$ teaspoon dried oregano
Freshly ground black pepper
1 teaspoon sesame seeds
$1/4$ cup olive oil
$1/4$ cup brown rice
2 tablespoons seasoned miso, such as
  South River Miso's Garlic Red Pepper

Pick through and wash the peas and lentils.
In a large pot, bring the water to a boil and
add the peas and lentils. Add the tomatoes,
carrots, garlic, and chiles. At this point you
can get creative with additional items such
as leeks, green peppers, and onions. Add the
lemon juice. Reduce the heat to a simmer
and add the basil, salt, oregano, pepper,
sesame seeds, and oil. Cook and cover for 20
minutes.

Add the rice and additional water if necessary. Cook for another 30 minutes, stirring
occasionally. Five minutes before comple-
tion, add the miso mixture.

Potato Leek–Miso Soup

Serves 2 to 4

Juice of 1 lemon
1 cup half-and-half
3 large potatoes, peeled and diced
4 large leeks, chopped
4 cups light miso broth
2 tablespoons chopped fresh dill
Salt

In a small bowl, combine the lemon juice
and half-and-half and set aside. Put the
potatoes, leeks, and miso broth in a large
pot and cook until the potatoes are tender,
about 20 minutes. Add the dill and salt to
taste and puree in a food processor or a
blender until smooth. Return the soup to
the pot, stir in the lemon mixture, and heat
through.

Note: You can be very inventive with the pea
and bean combination with excellent results.
Don't be afraid to try some of the Indian beans,
called dahls, such as toor dahl, chana dahl, or
urad dahl. Just use a total of $1^1/4$ to $1^1/2$ cups
dried beans.

Grains

Banana-Macadamia Pancakes with Orange Butter

Miso Porridge

Noachian Rice

Rice Pilaf

Spring Vegetables with Rice

Southwest Baked Millet

Whole-Wheat Linguine with Broccoli

Wild Rice Salad

Banana-Macadamia Pancakes with Orange Butter

Serves 2 to 4

Orange Butter

$^1/_2$ stick ($^1/_4$ cup) unsalted butter, softened
$^1/_2$ teaspoon finely grated orange zest
$1^1/_2$ teaspoons fresh orange juice
$^1/_8$ teaspoon salt

Pancakes

1 cup all-purpose flour
$^1/_2$ cup whole-wheat flour
2 tablespoons sugar
1 teaspoon baking powder
$^1/_2$ teaspoon baking soda
$^1/_4$ teaspoon salt
1 cup buttermilk
$^1/_2$ cup milk
2 tablespoons unsalted butter, melted
2 large eggs
1 teaspoon vanilla extract
1 ripe banana, cut into thin slices
$^1/_2$ cup macadamia nuts, chopped

To Make the Orange Butter In a small bowl, stir together all the ingredients until well combined. Use softened or put back in the refrigerator to harden. The butter will keep in the refrigerator for up to a week.

To Make the Pancakes In a large bowl, whisk together the flours, sugar, baking powder, baking soda, and salt. In another bowl, whisk together the buttermilk, milk, melted butter, eggs, and vanilla. Combine the wet and the dry ingredients along with the banana and the nuts.

Pour $^1/_4$ cup batter per pancake onto a hot buttered griddle. Cook until bubbles appear on the surface and the undersides are golden brown, 1 to 2 minutes. Flip and cook until the other sides are golden brown as well. Transfer to a large plate and loosely cover with foil (or a skillet lid) to keep warm, then make more pancakes, brushing the skillet with butter for each batch. Serve with orange butter and maple syrup.

Miso Porridge

Serves 2 to 4

2 cups water
1 cup rolled oats
$1/4$ cup chopped dates
$1/4$ teaspoon cinnamon
$1/4$ teaspoon cardamom
2 teaspoons light miso
Maple syrup

In a large saucepan, bring the water to a boil, add the oats and dates, and reduce the heat to low. Cook for 5 to 10 minutes, or until the water is absorbed. Let the oatmeal cool to body temperature and then thoroughly stir the spices and miso into the warm cereal. Cover and let sit overnight at room temperature (about 70°F.). In the morning, cook in the oven at 300°F. for 20 minutes or on the stove over low heat until warm. Serve with maple syrup.

Variations:

Try with other types of rolled, cracked, or ground grains. The dates could be replaced with raisins, currants, dried cranberries, or dried plums. The spices could include nutmeg, allspice, or extracts such as almond or hazelnut. Honey, molasses, or rice syrup could replace the maple syrup.

Noachian Rice

Serves 4 to 6

$1^1/2$ cups brown basmati rice
2 cups fresh corn kernels
2 cups dark kidney beans, cooked
1 zucchini squash, diced
1 yellow squash, diced
1 onion, diced
1 teaspoon cinnamon
Salt and freshly ground black pepper

Cook the rice according to the package directions and let cool. In a large bowl, fold the corn and beans into the rice. Put the diced vegetables, rice mixture, and cinnamon in a large skillet and sauté in olive oil until the vegetables have softened. Add salt and pepper to taste and serve hot.

Rice Pilaf

Serves 2 to 4

2$^1/_2$ cups chicken stock or
    vegetable stock
$^1/_4$ cup coarsely chopped blanched
    almonds
$^1/_4$ cup pine nuts
2 tablespoons extra-virgin olive
    oil or butter
1 medium onion, finely chopped
1$^1/_2$ cups long-grain rice
One 3-inch cinnamon stick
Salt and freshly ground black
    pepper
$^1/_4$ cup golden raisins, plumped in
    warm water

In a large pot, bring the stock to a slow
simmer. In a saucepan over medium heat,
gently sauté the almonds and pine nuts in
the oil. Stir constantly. When the nuts are
lightly browned, remove them from the
pan and set aside. Add the onion to the
pan and cook, constantly stirring, until
the onion is transparent but not brown,
about 10 minutes. Add the rice and continue to cook, stirring constantly, until the
rice has a light brown color, about 5 minutes. Add the hot stock and cinnamon stick
and season with salt and pepper to taste.
Stir in the rice until all the ingredients are
well mixed, then lower the heat and cover.
Cook until all the liquid is absorbed, 15 to
20 minutes. Remove from the heat and set
aside for 5 minutes. Stir in the sautéed
nuts and drained raisins. Remove the cinnamon stick before serving.

Spring Vegetables with Rice

Serves 4 to 6

1/4 cup extra-virgin olive oil
1 medium onion, chopped
3 large garlic cloves, crushed
1 red sweet pepper, cut into strips
1/2 pound small red potatoes, halved
1/2 cup drained canned tomatoes, cut in chunks
5 cups light miso stock or vegetable broth
Pinch of saffron
Salt and freshly ground black pepper
1/2 pound fresh green beans, cut into pea-size lengths
4 small artichokes, quartered
1 pound fresh fava beans, shelled
1/2 pound fresh green peas, shelled
1/2 pound fresh asparagus, trimmed and cut into 2-inch lengths
2 cups medium-grain rice

In a large saucepan, heat the oil over medium heat. Add the onion, garlic, and red pepper strips and cook until soft but not brown, about 15 minutes. Add the potatoes and tomatoes and cook for another 10 minutes, until the potatoes are just soft. Add the stock, saffron, and salt and pepper to taste. When the stock begins to boil, add the green beans and arti-chokes. Reduce the heat slightly, cover, and cook for 10 more minutes. Add the favas, peas, and asparagus. Add the rice and mix well. Cook until the rice is tender, 15 to 20 minutes. Remove from the heat and let stand for about 5 minutes. Adjust the seasonings and serve.

Southwest Baked Millet

Serves 6 to 8

2 cups millet
5 cups water
Pinch of salt
$1/2$ cup roasted sunflower seeds
$1/2$ teaspoon cumin
1 onion, diced
1 cup sweet corn
1 red bell pepper, diced
2 green chiles, seeded, ribbed, and minced
$1/4$ cup chopped or sliced black olives, plus
    additional for garnish
2 tablespoons South River Sweet-Tasting
    Brown Rice Miso
$1/2$ cup shredded jalapeño jack cheese

In a large pot, boil the millet with the water and salt for 40 minutes. The millet should be broken open. Remove from the heat and transfer to a casserole. Preheat the oven to 325°F. Add the rest of the ingredients, except for the cheese, and mix well to combine. Bake for 35 minutes. Top with cheese and additional black olives and bake for 5 to 10 more minutes.

Whole-Wheat Linguine with Broccoli

Serves 4 to 6

1 pound whole-wheat linguine
2 tablespoons olive oil
1 head of broccoli, trimmed and cut into
    small florets
3 garlic cloves, minced
$1/4$ teaspoon crushed red chile flakes
1 tablespoon tamari
$1/4$ cup grated Parmesan cheese or
    Asiago cheese
2 tablespoons toasted slivered almonds
Juice of 1 lemon
Salt and freshly ground black pepper

Bring a large pot of salted water to a boil. Cook the pasta for 7 to 9 minutes, until it is al dente. Drain and rinse in cold water. In a large sauté pan, heat the oil and sauté the broccoli florets over medium heat, stirring often, for 5 minutes. Add the garlic and the red chile flakes. Sauté for 1 minute longer. Add the cooked pasta to the broccoli and combine well. Add the tamari, cheese, and nuts. Add the lemon juice and season with salt and pepper to taste.

Wild Rice Salad

Serves 4 to 6

Sesame Ginger Dressing

$1/2$ cup plus 1 tablespoon toasted sesame oil
$1/4$ cup plus 2 tablespoons tamari
2 tablespoons brown rice syrup
$1/4$ teaspoon crushed red chile flakes
2 garlic cloves, minced
1 tablespoon grated fresh ginger

Salad

2 cups wild rice
$2^1/2$ cups water
1 medium red bell pepper, seeded and
    chopped
1 medium green bell pepper, seeded and
    chopped
1 small carrot, grated
1 cup toasted cashews
4 scallions, sliced thinly and on the diagonal

To Make the Dressing Puree the oil, tamari, brown rice syrup, red chile flakes, garlic, and ginger with a hand mixer or in a food processor or a blender.

To Make the Salad Place the rice and water in a covered saucepan and bring to a boil. Reduce the heat to a simmer, cover the rice, and cook over low heat for about 35 minutes, or until tender. Transfer the cooked rice to a large mixing bowl. While still warm, add the peppers, carrot, cashews, and scallions. Add the dressing and combine well. Serve at room temperature.

Vegetables

Avocado Skiffs

Pan-Roasted Cauliflower with
Pine Nuts and Raisins

Kinpira of Root Vegetables

Mushroom Sauce

Quick and Easy Oven-Grilled Asparagus

Roasted Vegetables

Roasted Butternut Squash

Simple Grated Carrot Salad

Delicious Mashed Potatoes

Vegetables with Mustard Vinaigrette

Avocado Skiffs

Serves 6

3 ripe avocados
Juice of $1/2$ lemon
1 cup diced fresh tomatoes, well drained
3 scallions, chopped
$1/4$ cup chopped fresh Italian parsley
1 tablespoon chopped fresh basil, or
    1 teaspoon dried basil
$1/8$ teaspoon dried rosemary
$1/4$ cup extra-virgin olive oil
1 small garlic clove, minced
Salt and freshly ground black pepper

Slice the avocados in half lengthwise and carefully
scoop out the flesh, discarding the pits and leaving the
shells intact. Coarsely chop the avocado flesh and place
it in a bowl. Sprinkle it with the lemon juice. Add the
tomatoes, scallions, parsley, basil, and rosemary, stirring
to combine. In a small bowl, whisk together the oil,
garlic, and salt and pepper to taste and pour over the
avocado-tomato mixture. Mound this mixture into
the avocado shells and serve.

Pan-Roasted Cauliflower with Pine Nuts and Raisins

Serves 4 to 6

$1/4$ cup raisins
4 tablespoons olive oil
1 head of cauliflower, florets trimmed and
    cut into 1-inch pieces, parboiled, and
    patted dry
4 garlic cloves, thinly sliced
$3/4$ teaspoon salt
$1/4$ cup pine nuts
$1/4$ teaspoon dried red chile flakes
$1 1/2$ cups tomato sauce
$1/2$ cup chicken stock
Pinch of saffron
2 tablespoons balsamic vinegar
1 tablespoon honey
$1/2$ teaspoon unsweetened cocoa powder

Macerate the raisins in hot water for 10 minutes. Drain
and set aside. In a skillet, heat 2 tablespoons of the oil
until it just begins to smoke. Add the cauliflower florets
and cook for 2 minutes. Add the garlic and cook for
2 minutes more. Stir well. Sprinkle with $1/4$ teaspoon salt
and transfer to a bowl. Wipe out the pan and add the
remaining 2 tablespoons oil. Over medium heat, cook
the raisins, pine nuts, and chile flakes for 4 minutes.
Add the cauliflower. Stir and cook for 3 to 4 minutes.
Add the remaining $1/2$ teaspoon salt, the tomato sauce,
stock, saffron, vinegar, honey, and cocoa. Bring to a boil.
Simmer until the sauce is absorbed, about 4 minutes,
and then serve.

Kinpira of Root Vegetables

Serves 4

2 teaspoons toasted sesame oil
1 cup julienned burdock root or parsnips
Pinch of salt
1 cup julienned carrot
1 cup thin half-moon slices lotus root or bamboo shoots
1-inch piece ginger, grated and squeezed for juice
Tamari
$^{1}/_{4}$ cup minced parsley

In a skillet, heat the oil over high heat and sauté the burdock root with the salt for about 2 minutes. Spread the burdock root evenly over the bottom of the skillet and top with the carrot and then the lotus root. Sprinkle the ginger juice over the top and add water to just cover the burdock. Reduce the heat to medium-low, cover, and cook for 10 minutes. Season lightly with the tamari, cover, reduce the heat to low, and cook until all of the liquid is absorbed, about 7 minutes. Stir gently to combine. Serve hot, garnished with parsley.

Mushroom Sauce

Serves 4

1 tablespoon peanut oil or toasted sesame oil
$^{1}/_{2}$ onion, chopped
2 tablespoons chopped parsley
$^{1}/_{2}$ cup sliced shiitake mushrooms
1 tablespoon arrowroot
2 tablespoons fresh ginger, grated and squeezed for juice
2 tablespoons tamari
1 teaspoon tahini

Heat the oil in a small saucepan and add the onion, parsley, and mushrooms. Cover the pan and sauté over low heat for 5 to 10 minutes, until the onions are translucent.

In a measuring cup, dissolve the arrowroot in 1 cup of water. Add the ginger juice and the tamari and stir. Slowly add the mixture to the cooked mushrooms and stir over low heat until the sauce thickens. Add the tahini and more water if the sauce is too thick.

Quick and Easy Oven-Grilled Asparagus

Serves 4

1 pound asparagus
2 tablespoons extra-virgin olive
   oil
Salt and freshly ground black
   pepper

Preheat the broiler. Snap off the tough
bottom part of the asparagus. On a cookie
sheet, line up the asparagus stalks and
drizzle with the oil. Sprinkle generously
with salt and pepper. Roll the asparagus
around a little to completely coat the
stalks. Broil for 5 minutes, watching carefully. Serve immediately.

Roasted Vegetables

Select a variety of root vegetables, including:

carrots
parsnips
turnips
beets
potatoes
Extra-virgin olive oil
Fresh or dried herbs such as
    parsley, rosemary, or thyme
    (chop finely if using fresh)
Salt and freshly ground black
    pepper

Preheat the oven to 425°F.

Peel and cut all the vegetables except the potatoes into thin slices. Cut the potatoes into chunks.

Spread the vegetables in a roasting pan or on a cookie sheet. Drizzle with oil and season with the herbs and salt and pepper to taste.

Roast the vegetables, stirring occasionally with a wooden spoon, for about 30 minutes, or until done.

Roasted Butternut Squash

Serves 4 to 6

1 medium butternut squash, peeled and
  cubed
2 medium onions, cut into small wedges
  about 1 inch wide
3 tablespoons canola oil
2 teaspoons salt
$1/2$ teaspoon ground nutmeg
$1/2$ teaspoon dried rubbed sage
$1/2$ teaspoon freshly ground black pepper
$1/8$ cup dried cranberries

Preheat the oven to 400°F. Place the squash in a mixing
bowl and add the onions, oil, salt, nutmeg, sage, and
pepper. Mix until the vegetables are well coated. Put the
mixture in a shallow baking pan. Roast, stirring occasionally, until the vegetables are tender and golden
brown, about 45 minutes. The squash should be firm,
not mushy. Remove the pan from the oven and add the
cranberries. Toss lightly to combine, and serve.

Simple Grated Carrot Salad

Serves 2 to 4

1 pound carrots, grated
3 tablespoons balsamic vinegar
1 bunch parsley leaves, chopped well

Combine the carrots, vinegar, and parsley in a bowl.
Taste and add more vinegar if desired. Chill thoroughly
before serving.

Delicious Mashed Potatoes

Serves 4 to 6

2¹/₂ pounds baking potatoes, cut in half
6 garlic cloves, peeled
¹/₃ cup extra-virgin olive oil
Salt and freshly ground black pepper

Bring a pot of salted water to a boil. Add the potatoes and garlic cloves and cook, covered, over medium heat until the potatoes are very tender, about 25 minutes.

Drain the potatoes and garlic and put them in a warm serving bowl. Using a potato masher, mash them coarsely, adding the oil a little at a time. When all the oil is added, taste and add salt and pepper. Serve immediately.

Vegetables with Mustard Vinaigrette

Steam or poach any one or a combination of the following vegetables:

Artichokes
Beets
Broccoli
Broccoli rabe
Chicory
Green beans
Leeks
Spinach

Vinaigrette

1 tablespoon Dijon mustard
2 tablespoons red wine vinegar
2 teaspoons sugar or honey
¹/₂ teaspoon salt
¹/₂ cup extra-virgin olive oil
¹/₄ teaspoon freshly ground black pepper
2 tablespoons fresh herbs such as parsley, chives, oregano, basil, or marjoram

1 tablespoon grated hard cheese such as Parmesan or manchego

To Prepare the Vinaigrette

In a bowl, whisk together the mustard and vinegar. Add the sugar and salt and mix again. Slowly add the oil, whisking continuously. Grind in the black pepper and stir in the herbs. Set aside.

When the vegetables are tender, drain them and return them to their cooking pan. Add the cheese. Toss the vegetables to mix and add enough vinaigrette to coat. Serve at room temperature.

Beans

Adzuki Beans and Delicata Squash

Bean, Corn, and Pumpkin Stew

Beans with Olive Oil and Lemon

Black Bean and Pepper Salad

Black Bean Chili

Skillet-Roasted Lima Beans with Herbs

Creamy White Beans

Vegetable and Bean–Stuffed Squash

Yellow Fava Beans and Rice

Adzuki Beans and Delicata Squash

Serves 2 to 4

1 cup adzuki beans, soaked overnight
1-inch piece kombu*
1 delicata squash, cut into rings
1 tablespoon extra-virgin olive oil
Salt and freshly ground black pepper
$1/2$ cup diced onion
4 tablespoons South River Adzuki Miso

In a saucepan over medium heat, cook the beans with the kombu and 2 cups of water for $1^1/2$ hours, adding more water as needed. Preheat the oven to 350°F.

Coat the squash with the oil and salt and pepper to taste. Bake for 35 minutes. When the beans are soft, add the onion and miso. Continue cooking until all the liquid is absorbed. When the squash is ready, stuff it with the beans, bake for an additional 15 to 20 minutes, and serve.

*Kombu is a thick, dark brown sea vegetable that lends itself to flavoring soups and broths. It enhances the flavor of beans.

Bean, Corn, and Pumpkin Stew

Serves 6 to 8

1 cup pinto beans, soaked overnight
Salt
1 teaspoon cumin seeds
1 teaspoon dried oregano
1-inch cinnamon stick
3 cloves
4 tablespoons light olive oil
1 large onion, diced
2 garlic cloves, minced
1 tablespoon paprika
1 pound fresh tomatoes, peeled and seeded, juice reserved
3 cups pumpkin puree
2 cups light miso broth
$1^1/2$ cups corn kernels
2 green chiles, seeded and minced
Chopped parsley, for garnish

In a saucepan, cover the beans with water. Add $1/2$ teaspoon salt and cook for $1^1/2$ hours. Drain the beans and reserve the cooking liquid.

Heat a small skillet and toast the cumin seeds until fragrant. Add the oregano, cook for 5 seconds, and transfer to a plate. Grind the seeds in a spice mill with the cinnamon stick and cloves. In a large saucepan, heat the oil and sauté the onion over high heat for 1 minute, then lower the heat to medium. Add the garlic, paprika, and 1 teaspoon salt. Stir to combine, then add $1/2$ cup of the reserved bean broth and cook, stirring occasionally. Next add the tomatoes and cook for 5 minutes. Then add the pumpkin and 1 cup of the miso broth and continue cooking. After 30 minutes, add the corn, beans, and chiles. Thin with the reserved tomato juice and the remaining miso broth. Cook until the pumpkin is heated through, 15 to 20 minutes. Adjust the seasonings and garnish with parsley.

Beans with Olive Oil and Lemon

Serves 2 to 4

2 cups beans, soaked overnight
2 garlic cloves, minced
1 teaspoon salt
$^1/_2$ cup fresh lemon juice
$^1/_4$ cup extra-virgin olive oil
$^1/_2$ cup flat-leaf parsley
6 scallions
1 lemon, cut into wedges

Drain the beans and place them in a saucepan. Cover with fresh water and bring to a boil over medium heat. Simmer until the beans are tender, 1 to 2 hours, depending on the bean. When they are done, remove from the heat, drain, and reserve the cooking liquid.

Mash the garlic with the salt until it forms a paste. Add the lemon juice and mix well. Remove 1 cup of the beans and mash them with $^1/_2$ cup of the reserved bean liquid. Mix with the garlic and add the rest of the beans. Stir in the oil and pour on a serving plate. Garnish with the parsley, scallions, and lemon wedges. Serve with bread.

Black Bean and Pepper Salad

Serves 4 to 6

$1^1/_4$ cups black beans, soaked overnight
1 bay leaf
$^1/_2$ teaspoon dried thyme
$^1/_2$ teaspoon dried oregano
1 teaspoon salt
$^1/_4$ cup vinaigrette
$^1/_2$ cup each red, yellow, and green bell
    pepper, diced small
$^1/_2$ red onion, finely chopped
1 celery stalk, diced small
1 green chile, seeded and minced
Chopped flat-leaf parsley, for garnish

In a saucepan, cover the beans with fresh water. Add the bay leaf and the herbs and bring to a boil. Add the salt, lower the heat, and simmer for 1 hour. Drain the beans.

Add the vinaigrette to the cooked beans while they are still warm, along with the peppers, onion, and celery. Stir everything together and adjust the seasonings. Add the minced chile. Garnish with parsley and serve at room temperature.

Black Bean Chili

2 cups black beans, soaked overnight
1 bay leaf
4 teaspoons cumin seeds
4 teaspoons dried oregano
4 teaspoons paprika
$^1/_2$ teaspoon cayenne pepper
3 tablespoons corn oil
3 onions, chopped
4 garlic cloves, chopped
$^1/_2$ teaspoon salt
3 tablespoons chili powder
1 (28-ounce) can whole tomatoes
1 to 2 teaspoons chopped chipotle chile
1 tablespoon rice wine vinegar
4 tablespoons chopped cilantro

Muenster cheese, grated
Sour cream
Canned green chiles, rinsed and diced
Chopped cilantro

Drain the beans and refresh the water. In a saucepan, bring them to a boil with the bay leaf. Lower the heat and let the beans simmer for 1 hour.

Meanwhile, add the cumin seeds to a dry skillet and roast over medium heat until they are fragrant. Add the oregano, paprika, and cayenne. Toast for a few seconds, then put into a coffee grinder or a spice mill to make a coarse powder.

In a large skillet, heat the oil and sauté the onions over medium heat until they soften, 3 to 5 minutes. Add the garlic, salt, oregano mixture, and chili powder and cook for another 5 minutes. Add the tomatoes and 1 teaspoon of the chipotle chile. Simmer for 15 minutes, then add the mixture to the beans with enough water to cover the beans by at least 1 inch. Cover and cook for 1 hour or longer, adding more water to keep the beans covered.

When the beans are cooked, taste them and add more chipotle if needed. Adjust the seasonings with vinegar, salt, and cilantro.

Serve the chili ladled over a large spoonful of grated cheese, and garnish with sour cream, green chiles, and cilantro.

Pan-Roasted Lima Beans with Herbs

Serves 4

1 pound frozen lima beans
2 teaspoons extra-virgin olive oil
2 large garlic cloves, minced
$^1/_4$ cup pitted, chopped green olives
$^1/_2$ teaspoon dried basil
$^1/_2$ teaspoon dried oregano
$^1/_4$ teaspoon dried sage
$^1/_4$ teaspoon freshly ground black pepper
$^3/_4$ cup canned diced roasted red peppers,
    well drained

Preheat the oven to 400°F.

In a large pot, cook the lima beans in enough boiling salted water to cover them until firm-tender, 8 to 10 minutes. Drain the beans and dry them on paper towels. Place the beans in a mixing bowl. Add the oil, garlic, olives, basil, oregano, sage, and pepper. Toss well.

Place the bean mixture in a single layer in a baking pan, spreading thinly and evenly. Roast, stirring occasionally, until the beans are softened and golden brown, 10 to 15 minutes. Remove from the baking pan and place in a serving bowl. Mix in the red peppers before serving.

Creamy White Beans

Serves 2 to 4

$^3/_4$ cup small white beans, soaked overnight
$^1/_2$ teaspoon salt
$1^1/_2$ cups thinly sliced onion
$^1/_2$ cup chopped celery
$^1/_2$ cup chopped celery leaves
$^1/_2$ cup chopped carrot
$^1/_2$ cup minced parsley
2 tablespoons olive oil
2 tablespoons butter
5 cups light miso broth
$^1/_2$ cup tomato paste
$^1/_2$ teaspoon dried basil
$^1/_2$ teaspoon white pepper
1 cup half-and-half
$^1/_2$ cup spinach cut into strips

In a saucepan, cook the beans in $1^1/_2$ cups of salted water for 1 hour, until tender. In a sauté pan over medium-low heat, sauté the vegetables and parsley in the oil and butter, covered, for 30 minutes. Do not allow to brown.

Add the broth, tomato paste, basil, pepper, and beans. Bring to a boil, add the half-and-half, and heat through. Reduce the heat, cover, and simmer for 1 hour, or until the beans are tender. Puree in a food processor or a blender. Return the soup to the pot and heat thoroughly. Adjust the seasonings. Serve in bowls with the spinach garnish.

Vegetable and Bean-Stuffed Squash

Serves 4 to 6

2 acorn squash
Salt
2 tablespoons extra-virgin olive oil, plus
  additional for rubbing the squash
1 medium yellow onion, chopped
1 medium carrot, sliced
1^1/$_2$ cups chopped kale
1 cup black beans, soaked overnight and
  cooked until tender
1 cup fresh corn kernels
^{1}/$_2$ teaspoon tamari
^{1}/$_2$ teaspoon cumin
^{1}/$_2$ teaspoon paprika
^{1}/$_2$ teaspoon freshly ground black pepper

Preheat the oven to 350°F.

Cut the acorn squash in half, scoop out the seeds, and rub with salt and a small amount of oil. Place the squash halves facedown on a baking pan. Roast until the flesh is tender, about 50 minutes.

While the squash is roasting, add the oil to a sauté pan and cook the onion until soft, about 3 minutes. Add the carrot and kale and cook for 2 to 3 minutes more. Add the black beans, corn, tamari, and spices and sauté until everything is tender, 10 to 15 minutes.

Once the squash is done baking, add the vegetable bean mixture and serve warm.

Yellow Fava Beans and Rice

Serves 6 to 8

1 cup yellow fava beans, soaked overnight
3 tablespoons extra-virgin olive oil
1 tablespoon turmeric
1 teaspoon cinnamon
^{1}/$_2$ teaspoon freshly ground black pepper
1 large onion, chopped
2 cups brown basmati rice
^{1}/$_4$ cup butter, melted
1 teaspoon salt
^{1}/$_2$ cup golden raisins
^{1}/$_2$ cup chopped dates
3 scallions, thinly sliced
1 lemon, cut into wedges

Drain the beans well. Heat 2 tablespoons of the oil in a 3-quart heavy nonstick saucepan over medium heat. Add the turmeric, cinnamon, and pepper and sauté for 1 minute. Add the onion and sauté for 15 minutes. Add the beans and 3 cups of water and bring to a boil. Lower the heat and simmer, covered, for 45 minutes.

Meanwhile, combine the rice and another 3 cups of water and let soak for 1 hour. Add to the beans. Cover and return to a boil. Reduce the heat and simmer for 20 minutes until all the water is absorbed.

Pour the butter and the remaining tablespoon of oil on top of the rice and beans. Cook on very low heat for 40 minutes. Remove and let cool for 5 minutes. Stir in the raisins and dates, being careful not to disturb the crust on the bottom. Remove the rice, a spoonful at a time, without breaking the crust. Mound the rice on a serving platter and garnish with scallions and lemon wedges. Remove the bottom crust. Slice and serve with the rice and beans.

Fish

Cod with Sautéed Vegetables

Ginger-Sesame Alaska Salmon

Oven-Braised Fish

Shrimp, Fennel, and Quinoa Pilaf

Smoked Trout with Farfalle and Rapini

Cod with Sautéed Vegetables

Serves 4

1 tablespoon extra-virgin olive oil
4 cod fillets, 4 to 6 ounces each
Salt and freshly ground black pepper
2 tablespoons butter
2 cups shredded carrots
1 cup shredded zucchini
1 cup sliced mushrooms
1/4 cup chopped green onion
1 garlic clove, minced
1 tablespoon sesame seeds
Lemon slices

Preheat the oven to 350°F.

Coat a baking dish with the oil and add the cod fillets. Season lightly with salt and pepper and bake for 20 minutes.

In a sauté pan, heat the butter over medium heat. Add the carrots, zucchini, mushrooms, green onion, garlic, and sesame seeds and sauté lightly until tender, 5 to 7 minutes.

When the cod is finished, top with the sautéed vegetables, garnish with lemon, and serve.

Ginger-Sesame Alaska Salmon

Serves 2 to 4

1 small onion, sliced into rings
2 medium carrots, shredded or julienned
1 1/2 pounds Alaska salmon fillet
2 teaspoons grated fresh ginger
2 tablespoons seasoned rice vinegar, plus
    additional to taste
2 teaspoons toasted sesame oil
Salt and freshly ground black pepper
Fresh spinach leaves

Preheat the oven to 325°F.

Add the onion and carrots to a small covered baking dish, just big enough to hold the salmon fillet. Top with the salmon. In a small bowl, combine the ginger, rice vinegar, and oil. Pour over the salmon. Season with salt and pepper to taste. Cover and bake for 20 minutes, or until the fish flakes easily when tested with a fork.

Serve the salmon topped with onion rings and carrots on a bed of spinach. Sprinkle with additional seasoned rice vinegar.

Oven-Braised Fish

Serves 4 to 6

1¹/₂ to 2 pounds fish steaks such as salmon, hake, or halibut, each about 1 inch thick
Flour for dredging
3 tablespoons extra-virgin olive oil
2 large onions, halved and thinly sliced
1 garlic clove, minced
2 bay leaves
1 teaspoon salt
¹/₂ teaspoon paprika
Juice of ¹/₂ lemon

Preheat the oven to 375°F.

Lightly dredge the fish steaks in a little flour, shaking them to remove any excess. In a sauté pan over medium heat, sauté the steaks in 2 tablespoons of the oil for 3 to 4 minutes on each side. Transfer to a glass baking dish and lay them flat, without overlapping. Add the onions, garlic, bay leaves, salt, and the remaining tablespoon of oil to the same sauté pan. Stir to mix well. Cover and cook for 15 minutes. Remove the bay leaves and add the paprika and lemon juice. Cover the fish with the onions and bake for 20 minutes.

Shrimp, Fennel, and Quinoa Pilaf

Serves 4

2 fennel stalks with fronds
3 tablespoons extra-virgin olive oil
1 medium onion, chopped
1 garlic clove, minced
¹/₂ teaspoon cayenne pepper
1¹/₄ cups quinoa, washed well
1 ripe tomato, peeled, seeded, chopped, and drained
2 cups water or chicken broth
2 teaspoons Worcestershire sauce
¹/₂ teaspoon salt
1 pound medium shrimp, peeled and deveined
Freshly grated nutmeg

Preheat the oven to 350°F.

Chop the fennel stalks and fronds separately. Set aside. In a 2-quart ovenproof casserole over medium heat, heat the oil. Stir in the onion, garlic, and cayenne, lower the heat, and sauté until the onion is tender, about 10 minutes. Add the fennel and quinoa and sauté for 2 minutes more. Add the tomato, water, Worcestershire sauce, and salt and bring to a simmer. Cover and bake for 25 minutes, or until the liquid is absorbed.

Remove from the oven. Uncover, fluff with a fork, and stir in the shrimp. Cover and let stand for 10 minutes. The heat will cook the shrimp. Sprinkle with nutmeg and chopped fennel fronds. Serve hot or at room temperature.

Smoked Trout with Farfalle and Rapini

Serves 6

2 bunches rapini or 2 large heads of broccoli
Salt
3 tablespoons extra-virgin olive oil
2 garlic cloves, minced
6 ounces smoked trout
1 small dried red chile, including seeds,
    chopped
1 pound farfalle
Freshly ground black pepper
Capers

Clean and roughly chop the rapini. In a large pot, bring
an inch of salted water to a boil. Add the rapini and
cook until only a few tablespoons of liquid are left in
the bottom of the pan, about 7 minutes. Set the pan
aside but keep warm.

In a sauté pan, heat the oil over medium heat. Add the
garlic and sauté until lightly brown. Add the trout and
mash gently into the garlic oil. Add the chile and mix
well. Combine with the rapini.

Cook the pasta in lightly salted boiling water until al
dente, 10 to 12 minutes. Drain the pasta and immediately combine with the rapini mixture. Transfer to a
warm serving bowl and season with freshly ground
pepper to taste. Sprinkle with capers and serve.

Meat and Poultry

Mushroom and Beef Stroganoff

Beef Stew

Chicken with Coconut-Curry Sauce

Chicken with a Miso-Honey Glaze

Chicken with Olive Rice

Chicken Sausage, Chard, and Beans over Polenta

Grilled Chicken in a Lemon Marinade

Stuffed Peppers

Mushroom and Beef Stroganoff

Serves 4 to 6

3 tablespoons olive oil
$^1/_2$ large onion, chopped
1 clove garlic, diced
$^1/_2$ cup burgundy wine
1 pound beef, cubed
1 pound white button mushrooms, sliced
2 portobello mushrooms, diced
$^3/_4$ cup oat milk or soy milk
3 tablespoons tamari
1 teaspoon freshly ground black pepper
2 bay leaves
1 tablespoon fresh thyme or 1 teaspoon
    dried thyme
1 pound cooked linguine

In a large sauté pan, heat the oil over medium-low heat.
Add the onion and garlic and cook slowly until brown,
about 5 minutes. Deglaze the pan with the wine as the
onion and garlic cook. Add the beef and sauté for
20 minutes at medium-low heat. Add the mushrooms
and sauté for 2 minutes, until the mushrooms are limp.
Add the oat milk, tamari, pepper, bay leaves, and thyme.
Simmer for 10 minutes; the mixture will thicken. Serve
over cooked linguine.

Beef Stew

Serves 6 to 8

1 pound stewing beef, cut into chunks
Whole-wheat flour for dredging
2 tablespoons extra-virgin olive oil
2 medium onions, chopped
4 cups mixed vegetables*
1 cup red wine
1 tablespoon fresh thyme
1 tablespoon fresh sage
1 tablespoon fresh oregano
$^1/_4$ cup chopped parsley
1 teaspoon salt
1 teaspoon freshly ground black pepper
2 potatoes, cut into chunks

Coat the stewing beef in whole-wheat flour and sauté
in the oil until browned. Add the onions to the pan and
cook for an additional 5 minutes. Add to a slow cooker
along with the seasonal vegetables (parsnips are an
excellent addition). Add the wine and 2 cups of water,
along with the chopped fresh herbs, salt, and pepper.
Cover and cook on low for 5 hours. Add the potatoes
and cook for another 1 to 1$^1/_2$ hours, until tender. Adjust
the seasonings. Serve with red wine and rustic bread.

*Use carrots, onions, parsnips, or any seasonal
vegetables.

Chicken with Coconut-Curry Sauce

Serves 2 to 4

1 cup unsweetened coconut milk
$1/4$ cup fresh lime juice
2 teaspoons lime zest
$1/4$ cup brown sugar or honey
$1/4$ cup chopped scallion
$1/4$ cup cilantro
2 teaspoons curry powder
$1/4$ teaspoon sea salt
$3^1/2$- to 4-pound whole chicken

Preheat the oven to 400°F.

Combine all the ingredients except the chicken in a bowl and whisk thoroughly. Coat the chicken with half of the mixture and place in a roasting pan with a rack. Roast for 1 hour. Baste with the remaining sauce. The chicken is cooked when an instant-read thermometer registers 170°F.

Chicken with a Miso-Honey Glaze

Serves 4

4 tablespoons South River Sweet-Tasting Brown Rice Miso
2 tablespoons honey
2 tablespoons apple cider vinegar
2 garlic cloves, minced
$1/2$ cup olive oil

2 large boneless chicken breasts, cut in half
Canola oil

To Prepare the Glaze Blend the miso, honey, vinegar, and garlic in a blender on high speed. Reduce the blender to medium speed and slowly add the oil to produce a thick, creamy glaze.

Place the chicken on a dish and cover thoroughly with the glaze. In a sauté pan, heat the oil over medium-high heat. Sauté the chicken on each side for $2^1/2$ minutes, then reduce the heat, cover, and simmer for 25 minutes until the juices run clear when the breasts are pricked with a fork.

Chicken with Olive Rice

Serves 4

2 tablespoons butter
$1/4$ teaspoon salt
$1/8$ teaspoon freshly ground black pepper
$1/2$ teaspoon dried thyme
$1/4$ teaspoon poultry seasoning
$1/4$ teaspoon paprika
Juice of 1 lemon
2 large boneless chicken breasts, cut in half

1 cup brown basmati rice
1 cup stuffed olives

Preheat the oven to 350°F.

In a sauté pan over medium heat, melt the butter. Add the seasonings and lemon juice and heat. Place the chicken in a baking pan and pour the lemon-butter mixture over the chicken. Bake for 1 hour. While the chicken is cooking, bring 2 cups of water to a boil and add the rice. Return to a boil, reduce to a simmer, cover, and cook for 20 to 30 minutes.

The chicken is cooked when the juices run clear when the breasts are pricked with a fork. When the chicken is done, pour off the juices into a measuring cup and skin off the fat. Add the remaining juices and olives to the rice. Serve the chicken pieces over the rice.

Chicken Sausage, Chard, and Beans over Polenta

Serves 4

3 tablespoons extra-virgin olive oil
1 onion, diced
2 garlic cloves, minced
Prepared polenta
2 chicken sausages, cooked and cut into pieces
1 can cannellini beans, soaked overnight and cooked until tender
1 small red bell pepper, roasted
5 whole cooked tomatoes
1 bunch Swiss chard, chopped
Basil
Parsley
Salt and freshly ground black pepper

In a large skillet, heat 1 tablespoon of the oil over medium heat. Add the onion and garlic. Sauté for 2 minutes until the onion is translucent and the garlic is lightly browned.

Preheat the oven to 250°F. Slice the polenta in $1/2$-inch-thick pieces. Heat another tablespoon of the oil in a large sauté pan over medium heat and sauté the polenta on both sides for $2^1/2$ minutes each until they are lightly browned. Once the polenta is finished, transfer the pieces to a plate and keep warm in the oven.

Cut the sausages into slices and cook in a sauté pan until browned, about 10 minutes. Transfer to a plate and keep warm in the oven. Heat the remaining tablespoon of oil in the same sauté pan over medium heat. Add the beans, pepper, tomatoes, chard, and seasonings. Cook until the chard is wilted and tender, about 10 minutes. Add the sausages to the mixture and serve over the warm polenta.

Grilled Chicken in a Lemon Marinade

Serves 5

1^1/$_2$ tablespoons white peppercorns
2 teaspoons cumin seeds
1 teaspoon coriander seeds
^{1}/$_2$ teaspoon cinnamon
12 garlic cloves
2 teaspoons salt
1 cup finely chopped onion
2 tablespoons grated lemon zest
^{1}/$_4$ cup fresh lemon juice
^{1}/$_4$ cup canola oil
^{1}/$_4$ cup chopped parsley
5 pounds chicken pieces

In a sauté pan over medium heat, toast the peppercorns, cumin, coriander, and cinnamon, stirring until fragrant, about 1 minute. Grind the spices. In a blender, puree the spices, garlic, salt, onion, lemon zest, juice, oil, and parsley. Put the marinade and chicken pieces in a ziplock bag and store in the refrigerator overnight.

Remove the chicken from the bag, allowing any excess marinade to drip away. Discard the balance of the marinade. Grill the chicken over medium heat for 25 minutes or bake at 325°F. for 30 to 40 minutes. The chicken is done when the juices run clear when pricked with a fork.

Stuffed Peppers

Serves 6

1 pound ground beef, ground lamb, or
    ground buffalo
2 tablespoons extra-virgin olive oil
1 medium onion, peeled and finely chopped
1 small can tomato paste
1 cup beef stock or vegetable stock
^{1}/$_2$ teaspoon dried thyme
^{1}/$_2$ teaspoon dried rosemary
^{1}/$_2$ teaspoon dried oregano
2 cups cooked brown rice
^{1}/$_4$ cup lightly toasted pine nuts
Salt and freshly ground black pepper
6 green bell peppers, stemmed, sliced in half
    lengthwise, and seeded
1 cup Parmesan cheese or Cheddar cheese

Preheat the oven to 350°F.

In a heavy skillet, brown the meat in the oil for 10 to 15 minutes. Add the onion, tomato paste, stock, and herbs. Bring to a boil and cook until the liquid has reduced by about half. Remove from the heat and stir in the rice, pine nuts, and salt and pepper to taste. Set the peppers in a buttered ceramic or glass dish, fill each pepper half with stuffing, and top with cheese. Bake for 45 minutes, until golden and bubbly.

Dairy

Cheese Soufflé

Basic Omelet

Pepper Quiche

Cheese Soufflé

Serves 6

6 tablespoons butter
6 tablespoons unbleached flour
1 cup cream mixed with 1 cup water,
    warmed
6 large eggs, separated, at room temperature
1 cup grated Gouda, Mahon, or Monterey
    Jack cheese
1 cup grated Parmesan cheese
Salt and freshly ground black pepper

Preheat the oven to 400°F.

In a heavy saucepan, melt the butter over medium heat. Add the flour and stir with a wooden spoon until the butter turns light brown. Gradually add the cream and water mixture, beating with a wire whisk until the mixture thickens. Remove from the heat and stir in the egg yolks, one at a time, and then the cheeses. Season with salt and pepper to taste. Place the egg whites in a glass or stainless-steel bowl and add a pinch of salt and beat until stiff. Gently fold the egg yolks into the egg whites and pour the mixture into a buttered 2-quart soufflé dish. Place in the preheated oven, lower the heat to 350°F., and bake for 40 minutes. Serve immediately.

Basic Omelet

Serves 2

4 large eggs at room temperature
Dash of hot sauce
Pinch of sea salt
2 tablespoons butter

Crack the eggs into a bowl. Add 3 tablespoons of water, the hot sauce, and salt and blend with a wire whisk. In a cast-iron skillet over medium heat, melt the butter. Add the eggs to the pan. Tip the pan to allow the eggs to cover the entire surface. Cook for several minutes over medium-low heat until the underside is lightly browned. Lift up one side with a spatula and fold the omelet in half. Reduce the heat and cook briefly, about 30 seconds. Slide the omelet onto a warm plate and serve.

Variation: Herb Omelet
Add 1 tablespoon finely chopped fresh herb, such as parsley, chives, dill, or thyme, into the egg mixture.

Pepper Quiche

Serves 4 to 6

I recommend purchasing whole-wheat pastry shells unless you're comfortable making your own piecrusts. You may use red, yellow, or orange peppers, or a combination.

1 prepared whole-wheat 9-inch piecrust
2 peppers, seeded and cut into thin strips
1 onion, finely sliced
2 tablespoons extra-virgin olive oil
3 large egg yolks
$1/2$ cup crème fraîche or heavy cream
Sea salt and freshly ground black pepper
1 cup freshly grated Parmesan cheese or
  Cheddar cheese

Preheat the oven to 350°F. Bake the piecrust for 20 minutes. Remove from the oven and let cool. Meanwhile, in a sauté pan over medium heat, sauté the peppers and onion in the oil until soft, about 6 minutes. Remove from the heat. In a mixing bowl, beat the yolks with the cream, seasonings, and half of the cheese. Spread the peppers over the baked crust and pour the egg mixture over. Top with the remaining cheese and bake for about 30 minutes, until golden.

Variation: Artichoke and Roasted Red Peppers or Sun-dried Tomatoes

Substitute $1/2$ pound sliced artichokes and $1/2$ cup either roasted red peppers or sun-dried tomatoes. Sauté in a mixture of 2 tablespoons butter and 2 tablespoons olive oil and proceed with the recipe.

Variation: Zucchini Quiche

Omit the peppers. Use 2 small zucchini, cut into thin strips. Mix with 1 tablespoon sea salt and drain in a colander for 30 minutes. Rinse and squeeze dry in a paper towel. Spread the zucchini over the baked crust and proceed with the recipe.

Desserts

Fresh Figs and Honey

Frozen Berry-Banana Parfait

Fruit Smoothie

Ginger-Pear Pie

Pears Poached in Vanilla Syrup

Quinoa and Date Pudding

Raspberry Custard

Rice Pudding

Fresh Figs and Honey

Serves 2 to 4

4 ounces ricotta
3 ounces cream cheese, softened
2 tablespoons milk
18 ripe figs
2 teaspoons chopped mint
Honey

In a bowl, beat together the ricotta, cream cheese, and milk until smooth. Chill in the refrigerator for 2 hours. Wipe the figs with a damp paper towel and slice off the stems. Cut a cross at the top to about $^{3}/_{4}$ inch. Squeeze at the base of the fig to open up the top. Spoon a bit of the cheese mixture into each fig. Sprinkle with mint and drizzle with honey. Serve on small plates or in dessert cups or bowls.

Frozen Berry-Banana Parfait

Serves 2

Berries in season are ideal. Otherwise, look for good frozen organic berries.

2 large bananas, peeled and frozen
2 tablespoons vanilla yogurt
1 teaspoon maple syrup
$^{1}/_{2}$ cup berries

Cut the bananas into chunks and puree with the yogurt and 2 tablespoons of water in a blender until creamy. Add the maple syrup and pulse again. Put a spoonful of berries in the bottom of two parfait glasses and top with about one-third of the banana mixture. Repeat the layers, ending with the berries. Serve immediately.

Fruit Smoothie

Serves 2

1 cup yogurt
1 cup orange juice
1 banana, frozen
$1/4$ fresh pineapple
1 apple
3 to 5 ice cubes

Put all the ingredients in a blender and blend until smooth. Add more juice if the liquid is too thick. Pour into glasses and serve.

Ginger-Pear Pie

Serves 4 to 6

Filling

5 cups sliced pears
3 tablespoons fresh lemon juice
$1/2$ cup sugar
2 tablespoons flour
1 teaspoon lemon peel
2 teaspoons minced fresh ginger

Topping

$1/2$ cup flour
$1/2$ cup sugar
$1/2$ teaspoon cinnamon
$1/8$ teaspoon mace
$1/4$ cup butter

10-inch prepared pie shell

Preheat the oven to 375°F.

To Make the Filling Sprinkle the pears with the lemon juice. In a bowl, combine the sugar, flour, lemon peel, and ginger and mix with the pears.

To Make the Topping In another bowl, cut together the flour, sugar, spices, and butter with two knives or a pastry cutter, until the mixture resembles coarse meal.

Put the pears in the pie shell and cover with the topping. Bake for 25 minutes with the edges covered and for another 25 minutes with the edges uncovered, until golden brown.

Pears Poached in Vanilla Syrup

Serves 6

1/2 cup sugar
1/2 vanilla bean, split lengthwise
3 1/2-inch strips lemon peel
6 firm pears, peeled, seeded, and cut in half

In a medium saucepan, bring 2 1/2 cups of water to a boil with the sugar, vanilla bean, and lemon peel. Stir to dissolve the sugar; then lower the heat and simmer for 2 to 3 minutes. Add the pears and cook them gently until they are translucent around the edges. Remove the pears from the syrup and put them in a bowl. Strain the syrup. Pour over the fruit and refrigerate until well chilled. Serve in individual dessert cups.

Quinoa and Date Pudding

Serves 4 to 6

3 tablespoons butter
Shortbread cookie crumbs
1/2 cup packed light brown sugar
2 large eggs, lightly beaten
1 cup milk
1 tablespoon vanilla extract
1 teaspoon cinnamon
Pinch of salt
2 cups cooked quinoa
1/2 cup chopped dates
1/2 cup toasted hazelnuts
Nutmeg

Preheat the oven to 325°F. Using 1 tablespoon of the butter, grease a 1 1/2-quart baking dish or individual ramekins. Coat the buttered surface with cookie crumbs. Set aside.

In a large bowl, cream the remaining butter and brown sugar. Stir in the eggs, milk, vanilla, cinnamon, and salt until blended. Add the quinoa, dates, and hazelnuts and mix thoroughly. Pour the custard mixture into a baking dish and grate a little nutmeg over the top. Bake for 50 minutes, or until just barely set. Remove from the heat and let cool for 10 minutes. To serve, spoon from the dish or loosen the edges with a knife and invert onto a serving plate.

Raspberry Custard

Serves 2 to 4

3 tablespoons cornstarch or arrowroot flour
1 quart milk
$1/2$ cup maple syrup
1 cup raspberries
Mint leaves

In a medium saucepan, dissolve the cornstarch in 3 tablespoons of water. Add to the milk along with the maple syrup and bring to a boil, stirring occasionally. Reduce the heat and simmer for 3 minutes. Cool slightly in a bowl and gently stir in the raspberries. Pour the pudding into individual custard cups and chill for 1 to 2 hours. Garnish with additional raspberries and mint leaves before serving.

Rice Pudding

Serves 4

1 quart milk
1 whole cinnamon stick (about 3 inches)
$1/2$ teaspoon crushed cardamom seeds
$1/8$ teaspoon whole cloves
1 cup white basmati rice
2 tablespoons almond butter
2 tablespoons honey
Pinch of salt

In a medium saucepan, bring the milk, cinnamon stick, cardamom seeds, and cloves to a boil. Add the rice, cover, and reduce the heat. Simmer for 1 hour. Discard the cinnamon stick and cloves. Stir in the almond butter, honey, and salt. Serve warm or chilled.

Acknowledgments

I would like to thank the following people who supported me with love and patience while I was working on this new venture:

First of all my family: my husband, Clifford, and our three children, John, Emilio, and Rossibel, for their presence in my life. Kelly Farrell for her nourishing meals and menus. A big thanks to my agent, Linda Roghaar, for encouraging me to "just do it," and to Tom Monte for putting my thoughts to paper. I could never have accomplished this project without the the professional and creative work of my coworkers at Dr. Hauschka Skin Care, Inc., who have created a fabulous team I'm proud to be part of. I would especially like to thank Mirran Raphaely, Betsy Strickland, Jill Price Marshall, Geoffrey Rice, Deborah Hubresch, Kathy White, and Robin Gingrass for finding time for all my last-minute requests. Thanks to Marie Hubonette for her friendship and contributions to the biography/life-cycle work that reminds us of the importance of each individual destiny. I'm forever grateful to Sandy Littell for her ceaseless commitment to the photo edits, and to Stacey Brosnan of Femsurge for her advice on topical treatments. Thanks to Sebastian Parsons for sharing his photos with us.

Thanks to WALA Heilmittel, the manufacturers of Dr. Hauschka Skin Care, for bringing the gift of holistic medicine and skin care to the world. I would especially like to thank Dr. Rudolf Hauschka for his pioneering work with natural substances and for his vision to bring a new business paradigm into the world. Thanks, too, to Karl Kossmann for helping to make Dr. Hauschka's dream a reality and for his willingness to share his experiences with me in wonderful interviews.

I cannot thank Elisabeth Sigmund enough for devoting her life to developing products and a therapeutic treatment for the contemporary woman on a path to self-knowledge. I dedicate this book to Elisabeth, and look forward to continued collaboration.

I am most grateful to Rudolf Steiner for anthroposophy, his great gift to the world. It is a source of daily inspiration for those of us working to awaken beauty.

Index

A

Acne, 97, 99–100
Acne rosacea, 102
Acupuncture, 108
Affirmation, morning, 123–25
Agriculture, biodynamic, 38, 44
Agriculture, sustainable, 38, 142
Alchemy, 105–17
   aging process, 110
   life cycles, 111–17
   life forces and, 105–9
Alcohol, 60
Aloe vera, 76
Alpha hydroxy acids (AHA), 55, 68–69
Ames, Bruce, 42
Anger, 17
Anthyllis, 48
Antioxidants, 39–42, 56
Astral body, 112
Avocado mask, 82

B

Bacteria, intestinal, 61–62
Baths
   expressing gratitude in, 108
   healing, 130–33
   lavender, 29, 49, 130
   lemon, 31, 99, 130
   restorative, 21–23
   rosemary, 33, 130
   spruce, 30, 130
Beans, 122
Beta carotene, 41
Biodynamic farming, 38, 44
Biodynamic food, 120, 141–42
Biography exercise, 137–38
Breakfast, 7-Day Menu, 147
Breakfast, healing, 127
Bryophyllum, 48
Burdock root, 76

C

Calendula, 49

Calories, 45
Cancer, 42
Cellulite, 57
Chamomile, 49, 76
Cheeks, 86, 91
Chi, 69, 106, 107–9
Chin, 89, 92
Choleric temperament, 29, 130
Cleansers
   for acne, 100
   cleansing the face, 70–74
   for dry skin, 101
   evening care, 130
   morning care, 125
   for oily skin, 99
   for rosacea, 97
Cold, common, 17
Collagen, 56
Constipation, 61

D

Dance, 108
Dermis skin layer, 56–57
Diaries, 20, 135
Diet. *See* Food
Digestive system, 58–62, 89
Dinner, 7-Day Menu, 147
Dinner, healing, 128–29
Doing "nothing," 18, 136
Dr. Hauschka products
   Body Wash Fresh, 77
   Clarifying Toner, 99, 100
   Cleansing Clay Mask, 100
   Cleansing Cream, 74, 99, 100, 101
   Cleansing Milk, 99, 100, 101, 102
   Facial Steam Bath, 100, 101
   Facial Toner, 78, 101
   Firming Mask, 102, 103
   Lemon Bath, 99, 100
   Moisturizing Day Cream, 83, 101
   Moisturizing Mask, 101
   Normalizing Day Oil, 83, 99, 100, 103
   Quince Day Cream, 83, 101
   Rejuvenating Mask, 101, 102, 103

Rhythmic Conditioner, Sensitive, 102
Rhythmic Night Conditioner, 84, 99, 100, 101, 135
Rose Day Cream, 83, 101, 102
Toned Day Cream, 83, 101
Translucent Bronze Concentrate, 100, 103

E

Echinacea, 76
Elastin, 56
Emotions, on face, 65–66
Emoto, Masaru, 21
Epidermis skin layer, 54–55
Essential oils. See Oils, essential
Etheric energy, 106, 107–9
Eurythmy, 26, 108
Exercise, physical, 25–26, 30, 60. See also Walking
Exercise, rhythmic, 108
Exercise, zen, 27
Exercises, facial, 90–93
Exfoliants, 71–74
Exhaustion, 16–17, 59
Eyebags, 86–87
Eye care, 126

F

Facial masks
    for acne, 97, 100
    for advanced rosacea, 103
    for dry skin, 101, 102
    evening care, 134
    homemade, 82
Facial skin, 65–93
    cleansing basics, 70–74
    common skin conditions, 95–96
    dry skin, 95, 101–3
    emotions expressed on, 65–66
    exercising muscles of, 90–93
    forehead region, 85
    four pillars of beauty, 67
    holistic vs. conventional skin care, 68–69
    homemade formulas for, 97
    lower region, 89

middle region, 86–87
    moisturizing basics, 78–83
    morning skin care, 125–27
    night care basics, 84
    oily skin, 95, 98–100
    toner basics, 75–78
Farming. See Agriculture
Fats, dietary, 47, 87
Fear, 17
Fertility, 142
Fertilizers, 142
Fiber, 61
Flavonoids, 43
Food
    biodynamic, 120, 141–42
    cravings, 47
    fermented, 61–62
    highest-quality, buying, 44, 120, 122–23
    organic, 44–45, 120, 141–42
    preparation tips, 121
    processed, 44, 46, 47, 87, 120
Footbaths, 132, 133
Forehead, 85, 90–91
Four Temperaments, 28–33, 130
Free radicals, 39, 56, 96
Fruits, 39, 42

G

German chamomile, 49
Goldenseal, 76
Goodness, 67
Grains, whole, 121, 127
Gratitude, expressing, 108
Greens, 121, 123

H

Hair care, 136–37
HALT emotions, 17
Healers, nonjudgmental, 19–20
Healing agriculture, 142
Healing beauty, practicing, 19–20
Healing practices, reinforcing, 20–21
Health care, 120
Heart health, 87
Herbal skin cleansers, 72–74

Herbal toners, homemade, 75–76
Herb-infused vinegar toners, 76
Holistic skin care, 68–69
Honey mask, 82
Humectants, 81

I
Immune system, 39–40, 54–55, 111
Indoles, 43
Inflammation, 39–40, 54–55
Isoflavones, 43

J
Journaling, 135, 137–38

K
Kidney health, 58–62, 86–87

L
Lavender oils, 22, 29, 49, 76, 102, 103, 130
Laxatives, natural, 61
Lemon, 50
Lemon oils, 22, 31, 130
Life cycle exercise, 137–38
Life force or energy, 105–9
Lips, 89
Love, 67, 108
Lunch, 7-Day Menu, 147
Lunch, healing, 128
Lung health, 86
Lymph system, 56–57, 58

M
Martial arts, 26, 28
Masks. See Facial masks
Massage, 20, 69, 108, 136
Mealtime rituals, 28, 47
Meditation, 27–28, 123–25, 135
Melancholic temperament, 32–33, 130
Melanocytes, 55
Menopause, 116
Menu, 7-Day, 147
Millet, 127
Miso, 122
Moisturizers, 78–83, 101, 126
Morning meditation and affirmation, 123–25
Morning skin care, 125–27

Music, 109

N
Nature walks, 24, 29, 67, 107–8, 136
Neck muscle exercises, 92–93
Nervous system, 58
Night care, facial, 84
Night care, healing, 130, 135
Nose, 87
Nutrients, in soil, 37–38

O
Oats, 122
Oils, essential, 22–23, 126. See also specific oils
Order, creating, 18
Organic agriculture, 38
Organic food, 44–45, 120, 141–42
Oxidants. See Free radicals
Oxidation, 39–40, 56
Oxygen Radical Absorbency Capacity (ORAC) scale, 39, 42

P
Perimenopause, 115
Philtrum, 89
Phlegmatic temperament, 31, 130
Plants, 35–51
    antioxidants in, 40–42
    in daily diet, 44–47
    for healthy skin, 48–51
    impact on health and beauty, 40–43
    soil quality and, 37–38
Practicing Beauty Program, 119–38
    benefits of, 119
    celebrating, at month-end, 138
    food preparation tips, 121
    highest-quality foods for, 120, 122–23
    skin care products for, 122
    twelve steps, 123–38
Precepts of the day, 123–24
Pritikin, Robert, 45
Processed food, 44, 46, 47, 87, 120
Protein, 60, 87

Q
Quinoa, 127

R

Rhythmic system, 58
Rice, 122
Rituals, mealtime, 28, 47
Rosacea, 97, 102, 103
Rosemary, 50, 76
Rosemary oils, 22, 33, 50, 130
Rhythms, internal, 15–33
    discovering, 18
    Four Temperaments, 28–33
    living against, signs of, 16–17
    meditation, 27–28
    nature walks, 24
    physical exercise, 25–26
    practicing healing behaviors, 19–20
    reinforcing healing behaviors, 20–21
    restorative baths, 21–23
    zen exercise, 27

S

Sage, 50
Sage oils, 23, 100
Saint-John's-wort, 51
Salt, sea, 60
Salutogenesis, 19, 57
Sanguine temperament, 30, 130
Saponins, 43
Sauna, 60
Sebum, 55, 57, 70, 71, 98, 99
Seven-grain cereal, 127
Skin, 53–62. See also Facial skin
    dermis layer, 56–57
    digestive health and, 61–62
    epidermis layer, 54–55
    functions performed by, 53, 58
    healing plants for, 48–51
    kidney health and, 59–60
    skin care products, buying, 122
    subcutaneous layer, 57
Sleep, 59
Sodium, 60
Soil quality, 37–38
Spelt, 127
Spruce oils, 23, 30, 33, 102, 130

Squash, 123
Sterols, 43
Strawberry yogurt mask, 82
Stress, 17
Subcutaneous skin layer, 57
Surfactants, 76
Sustainable agriculture, 38, 142
Sustainable beauty, 141–42
Sweat, 57, 60

T

Tai chi chuan, 26, 28
Throat exercises, 92–93
Toners
    for acne, 100
    applying, 75
    for dry skin, 101
    evening care, 130
    homemade, 75–76
    morning care, 126
    for oily skin, 99
Truth, 67

V

Vegetables, 39, 42
Vinegar-based toners, 76
Vitamin C, 41
Vitamin E, 42

W

Walking, 24, 26, 29, 60, 62, 107–8, 128, 136
Water, pure spring, 59, 61, 85
Weekend, healing, 135–37
Weight loss, 45–47
Witch hazel, 51
Writing, therapeutic, 20, 135, 137–38

Y

Yarrow, 76
Yoga, 26, 28

Z

Zen exercise, 27

Index of Recipes

B

Bean(s)
Adzuki, and Delicata Squash, 174
Black, and Pepper Salad, 175
Black, Chili, 176
Chicken Sausage, and Chard over
Polenta, 190
Corn, and Pumpkin Stew, 174
Lentil-Mushroom Stew, 153
Lentil-Spinach Soup, 153
Lima, Pan-Roasted, with Herbs,
178
Mixed-Pea Soup, 154
Noachian Rice, 159
with Olive Oil and Lemon, 175
and Rice, Greek Olive Soup with,
152
and Roasted Root Vegetable Soup,
150
Spring Vegetables with Rice, 161
and Vegetable-Stuffed Squash,
179
White, Creamy, 178
Yellow Fava, and Rice, 179
Beef
and Mushroom Stroganoff, 188
Stew, 188
Stuffed Peppers, 191

C

Chicken
with Coconut-Curry Sauce, 189
Grilled, in a Lemon Marinade, 191
with a Miso-Honey Glaze, 189
with Olive Rice, 190
Sausage, Chard, and Beans over
Polenta, 190

D

Dairy. *See* Eggs; Quiche

Desserts
Fresh Figs and Honey, 198
Frozen Berry-Banana Parfait, 198
Fruit Smoothie, 199
Ginger-Pear Pie, 199
Pears Poached in Vanilla Syrup,
200
Quinoa and Date Pudding, 200
Raspberry Custard, 201
Rice Pudding, 201

E

Eggs. *See also* Quiche
Basic Omelet, 194
Cheese Soufflé, 194
Herb Omelet, 194

G

Grains
Banana-Macadamia Pancakes
with Orange Butter, 158
Miso Porridge, 159
Noachian Rice, 159
Quinoa and Date Pudding, 200
Rice Pilaf, 160
Rice Pudding, 201
Shrimp, Fennel, and Quinoa Pilaf,
183
Southwest Baked Millet, 162
Spring Vegetables with Rice, 161
Whole-Wheat Linguine with
Broccoli, 162
Wild Rice Salad, 163

Q

Quiche
Artichoke and Roasted Red
Peppers, 195
Artichoke and Sun-Dried
Tomatoes, 195
Pepper, 195
Zucchini, 195

S

Salad, Black Bean and Pepper, 175
Salad, Grated Carrot, Simple, 170
Salad, Wild Rice, 163

Seafood
Cod with Sautéed Vegetables, 182
Ginger-Sesame Alaska Salmon,
182
Oven-Braised Fish, 183
Shrimp, Fennel, and Quinoa Pilaf,
183
Smoked Trout with Farfalle and
Rapini, 184
Soups
Bean and Roasted Root Vegetable,
150
Butternut Squash Bisque, 150
Curried Broccoli, 151
Greek Olive, with Beans and Rice,
152
Green, 152
Lentil-Spinach, 153
Mixed-Pea, 154
Potato Leek-Miso, 154
Stew, Bean, Corn, and Pumpkin, 174
Stew, Beef, 188
Stew, Lentil-Mushroom, 153

V

Vegetable(s)
Avocado Skiffs, 166
and Bean-Stuffed Squash, 179
Delicious Mashed Potatoes, 171
Mushroom Sauce, 167
with Mustard Vinaigrette, 171
Pan-Roasted Cauliflower with
Pine Nuts and Raisins, 166
Quick and Easy Oven-Grilled
Asparagus, 168
Roasted, 169
Roasted Butternut Squash, 170
Roasted Root, and Bean Soup,
150
Root, Kinpira of, 167
Simple Grated Carrot Salad, 170
Spring, with Rice, 161

Photo Credits

Art and Commerce, William Abranowicz: 131

Tara Baxter: 90, 91, 93

Sandra Costantini: 46 (below), 123, 125

Digital Vision, Veer: 18 (above), 73, 100 (below), 113

Furnald/Gray: 4, 7, 8 (above), 8 (center), 8 (below left), 13, 15, 16, 17, 22 (left), 24, 25, 36, 37, 38, 42, 43, 47, 50 (right), 51 (left), 55 (below), 65, 66, 67, 74, 86 (below), 95, 104, 105, 122 (above), 141, 143

Getty Images, Amy Neunsinger: 114

Getty Images, Botanica, Jennifer Cheung: 60 (above)

Getty Images, FoodPix, Sang An: 150

Getty Images, FoodPix, Benjamin F. Fink, Jr.: 192

Getty Images, FoodPix, Rob Fiocca: 160, 180

Getty Images, FoodPix, Richard Jung: 163, 196

Getty Images, FoodPix, Alison Miksch: 39

Getty Images, FoodPix, Ngoc Minh Ngo: 168

Getty Images, FoodPix, Lisa Romerein: 154

Getty Images, FoodPix, Mark Thomas: 146, 156, 177

Getty Images, FoodPix, Simon Watson: 185, 201

Getty Images, FoodPix, Cheryl Zibisky: 164

Getty Images, The Image Bank, Jean Louis Batt: 2

Getty Images, The Image Bank, Jason Homa: 139

Getty Images, The Image Bank, Rita Moss: 148

Getty Images, The Image Bank, Roger Wright: 85

Getty Images, Photonica, Neo Vision: 172

Getty Images, Stone Collection, April: 52

Getty Images, Stone Collection, Brian Bailey: 126

Getty Images, Stone Collection, Judith Haeusler: 120

Getty Images, Stone Collection, Bob Thomas: 144

Getty Images, Stone Collection, Jerome Tisue: 63

Getty Images, Taxi, Robin Macdougall: 186

Paul S. Grand: 46 (above)

Image100, Veer: 119, 122 (below)

Lightworks: 70, 71, 76

Sandy Littell: 19, 23 (right), 28, 33

Amy Neunsinger: 6

Photo Alto, Veer: 26, 61, 108

Photodisc, Veer: 40, 44, 133

Photography by Janine Hosegood for Cape Photographic / Elysia Natural Skin Care: 18 (below), 23 (left), 78 (below), 79, 80, 96

Deniz Saylan: 14, 34, 55 (above), 60 (below), 64, 69, 86 (above), 88, 110, 117, 118, 136, 140

Jonathan Sherrill: 32, 101, 107

Phil Stiles: 9 (above), 10

Courtesy of WALA Heilmittel GmbH: 8 (below right), 9 (below), 22 (center), 22 (right), 35, 48, 49, 50 (left), 50 (center), 51 (right), 53, 56, 57, 58, 77, 78 (above), 87, 94, 98, 100 (above), 103, 106, 132, 134